TIPPOO TIB

TIPPOO TIB.

TIPPOO TIB

THE STORY OF HIS CAREER IN CENTRAL AFRICA

NARRATED FROM HIS OWN ACCOUNTS

BY

DR. HEINRICH BRODE

AND TRANSLATED BY

H. HAVELOCK

WITH A PREFACE BY

SIR CHARLES ELIOT, K.C.M.G.

AFRO-AM PRESS
DIVISION OF AFRO-AM BOOKS, INC.
CHICAGO
1969

Library of Congress Catalog Card Number 78-99351

Standard Book Number 8411-0022-5

The original edition of this work was published
in London in 1907 by Edward Arnold. The copy from
which this reprint edition was made was loaned to
Afro-Am Press from the collections of Columbia
University Libraries

Manufactured in the United States of America by
RCS Press, Inc., Chicago

PREFACE

THE name of Tippoo Tib is familiar to all who took
an interest in the affairs of East Africa or the Congo
fifteen or twenty years ago. He was the most
remarkable of the band of Arab traders and explorers who, starting from the East Coast, penetrated to the Congo, and were the rulers of whatever country they happened to be in, though they
established no states and did not even claim the
right of conquest on behalf of their Sovereign, the
Sultan of Zanzibar. It is curious to notice how
much and how little they effected. They traversed
enormous distances, and demonstrated the practica-
bility of many routes through savage kingdoms which
were commonly considered pathless wildernesses;
but they made no attempt to attach these regions
to Zanzibar, or even to convert them to Mohammedanism.

The whole history of the Arabs in East Africa
shows the same characteristics. They founded their
cities on the coast, but made little effort to move
inland, and in the rare cases where they did so, as
at Tabora and Ujiji, the reason was simply that
their slave-raids had depopulated the region near
the sea, and they were forced to move on to districts
where the game was not so shy. But their terri-
torial and political instincts were feeble. The
effective power of the Sultan rarely extended more
than ten miles inland from the shore of the mainland. Beyond that limit, every Arab assumed the

v

right to deal with the natives exactly as he pleased. But, however successful he might be, he did not extend the Sultan's authority, and if he perished, the Sultan did not feel called on to avenge his death.

Dr. Brode, who has had exceptional opportunities for studying the career of Tippoo Tib, published some time ago in the 'Proceedings of the Institute of Oriental Languages' his autobiography, transcribed in Roman letters from his own manuscript, and accompanied by a translation. This work is now supplemented by a biography giving a connected chronological account of this adventurous career, which is worth reading both as a story and as a valuable addition to the obscure and scanty records of African history.

Its hero, Hamed bin Muhammed, better known by his nickname of Tippoo Tib, was of mixed Arab and negro descent, and the latter strain showed itself markedly in his physiognomy. Still, according to the ideas of Zanzibar, he was an Arab. Few dates are mentioned in his life until near the end. Arabs rarely know their ages exactly or keep any accurate diary. He was born in Zanzibar, and at the age of about eighteen went on a journey to Ujiji with his father, and continued it by himself to Urua, thus inaugurating the long series of trading expeditions which formed the occupation of his life. The chief objects of these expeditions were slaves and ivory. Ivory was plentiful, and the natives, who had often no notion of its value, were ready to sell it absurdly cheap. If they made difficulties, vigorous measures were adopted without scruple or hesitation. The journey to Urua was succeeded by another to Urungu, at the southern end of Tanganyika, in the course of which Tippoo Tib met Livingstone near Lake Mueru.

These were comparatively short journeys, but
Tippoo Tib now proceeded to make a much more
serious expedition, which was the foundation of his
influence and importance. He seems to have started
about 1867, and was away some fifteen years. Most
of this time was spent in what is now the territory
of the Congo Free State. There were Arab settlements in these regions, for the great distance from
Zanzibar and the necessity of having some fortified
centre and base of operations had obliged the
traders to depart somewhat from their habits of
predaceous migration. We hear that their headquarters—Nyangwe—was a considerable town, with
so many rice-fields round it that it was called New
Bengal. His doings during this long absence are
described in considerable detail. Part of the time
he bore the title of Sultan of Utetera.

According to his own account, he claimed the
sultanate in virtue of a perfectly fictitious relationship between his mother and the local royal family,
with the result that the reigning Sultan resigned
peacefully in his favour the day after he arrived.
One cannot help suspecting that there is some slight
lacuna in the narrative here. During this period
he met Cameron, and also Stanley, whom he guided
for a part of his journey towards the end of 1876.
After parting from Stanley, he again spent some
time in warring and trading, both in Kassongo and
Tabora. He met Wissmann, and escorted him to the
coast, and, as Dr. Brode says, if anything can justify
his life it is that he was a faithful guide to Cameron,
Stanley, and Wissmann, and had no small share in
their success, though it must be admitted that his
relations with these eminent explorers were not
unruffled.

His relations with Stanley were renewed in 1887.

After returning to Zanzibar in 1882, he went back to Utetera, but after a short absence was summoned home again by the Sultan. When Stanley organized his mission for the relief of Emin, he invited Tippoo Tib to accompany him as guide, and, on behalf of the King of the Belgians, offered him the title of Governor of certain provinces of the Congo Free State. Details of this expedition, which was Tippoo Tib's last important performance, are given in the biography.

It must be admitted that Tippoo Tib was a slave-trader. These pages, based upon his own statements, give some inkling of the unscrupulous cruelty with which he dealt with natives, and clearly much remains untold. In excuse, one can only say that the cruelty of the slave-traders was not greater than the cruelty of the natives to one another. One eminent Arab, when criticized by Europeans for his slave-trading propensities, used to relate how he had fallen in with a tribe who were accustomed to eat their prisoners of war. He bought all these prisoners for a small sum, and made them his slaves, which he maintained, with a logic difficult to controvert, was far better for them than the other fate. Still, no doubt Tippoo Tib's commercial journeys were in the main plundering expeditions. Anything else, any introduction of law and order, any spread of civilization, was merely subsidiary and incidental. But he was intelligent, not wantonly brutal, as many traders were ; he had a far better idea of organizing a rough-and-ready administration than most Arabs, and he was always friendly to Europeans. By the assistance which he rendered to them he indirectly contributed in no small measure to the civilization of Africa, for which the Arabs themselves have done so little.

He was practically King of an enormous territory,
but his power was never officially recognized even
by his own Sovereign. Had it been, the future of
East and Central Africa might have been materially
changed, for the chief argument advanced by the
European Powers who appropriated the hinterland
behind the coast was that the Sultan had no
effective jurisdiction over the natives there. But,
as Dr. Brode points out, Seyyid Burghash, the
Sultan of the period, had no talent or inclination
for politics, and cared only for trade in its crudest
aspects. He wished to get as much ivory as possible
from the interior, but he did not care anything
about the position and character of the countries
which produced it. Yet perhaps pessimism rather
than stupidity was the motive of his conduct.
'Hamed,' he said to Tippoo Tib, ' be not angry with
me ; I want to have no more to do with the mainland. The Europeans want to take Zanzibar here
from me ; how should I be able to keep the mainland ?' And Tippoo Tib adds : ' When I heard
those words I knew that it was all up with us.' It
certainly was. The Sultan's dominions on the mainland soon became little more than a legal fiction,
and he retains Zanzibar only on condition of also
accepting the doubtful blessing of British protection.

The disappearance of the Arabs from East and
Central Africa can hardly give cause for regret.
They were seen at their best in such men as our hero,
who, if he had had a free hand, might have established a firm if somewhat rapacious Government.
But, on the whole, they were merely a nation of
slave-traders, without much dignity or romance, and
illustrated the demoralizing effect of slavery on the
slave-owner. In the towns on the coast, where
they had plantations, and in the island of Zanzibar,

cultivation was kept up by a wasteful profusion of slave labour ; but they were careless of the interior, though they knew its good points and potentialities far better than Europeans. For administration, development, even for conquest, they showed a complete apathy. They cared for nothing but the simple right to help themselves to valuables when and how they chose. They were destructive, and did not even preserve any good that they might find in native institutions. Had they retained any considerable tract of country, such beneficial legislation as the abolition of the slave-trade, and the prohibition to import alcohol and weapons within a certain zone, would probably have proved impossible.

I used to see Tippoo Tib occasionally when I was His Majesty's Agent and Consul-General in Zanzibar in 1901 and 1902. His features were of the negro type, and produced at first an impression that he was a low-caste hybrid ; but this impression was dispelled by his polite and dignified manners and his flow of speech. The tremulous twitching of his eyelids was very noticeable, and it was generally believed that this was the origin of his name Tippoo Tib, 'the blinker,' although he himself, not liking the personal allusion, had other explanations. The touch of mockery in his manner and language, to which Dr. Brode more than once alludes, was very noticeable, but not unpleasant nor discourteous. He did not live to execute the journey to Europe which Dr. Brode tells us he was planning, but, not long ago, in the language of Mohammedanism, he removed to 'the abode of permanency,' though some Hindu cycle of transmigration would seem more congenial to such a wanderer and explorer.

C. ELIOT.

AUTHOR'S PREFACE

HAVING been resident for a considerable time in Zanzibar, I had the opportunity of becoming closely acquainted with the hero of this work, and I succeeded in inducing him to recount the story of his life, which seemed to me of interest in view of the important part which he has played in the history of African exploration. His descriptions were set down by him in Swahili in Arabic characters, and by me transcribed into Roman script, in which form they appeared, together with a German translation, in the 'Proceedings of the Institute of Oriental Languages,' Part III., fifth and sixth yearly issues.

In the preface of that study I pointed out that its publication in that place primarily served a linguistic purpose, and announced that I intended to work up the material furnished me by Tippoo Tib into a work on his life which should be generally intelligible.

The present book is the carrying out of that announcement. Owing to urgent professional work, its publication has been delayed longer than I anticipated. Within the framework of the life-history of a prominent personality it has been my object to lay before the reader, even though unfamiliar with African affairs, a picture of the varying fortunes of the Dark Continent before it gradually fell into European hands. The historical introduction in the first chapter may seem to many far-fetched, yet in the interest of the work as a whole I was loth to omit it. Should any reader find it wearisome, I beg him to begin at the second chapter, but whoever does not shrink from the trouble of reading it through will find in it many a hint which will make the subsequent descriptions more comprehensible.

Before the work leaves my hands I feel it my duty to express my thanks to all those who have afforded me their counsel and co-operation during its compilation.

THE AUTHOR.

ZANZIBAR,
September, 1903.

[The death of Tippoo Tib since the original edition was published has necessitated the addition of a few words by the author, which will be found on p. 253.]

CONTENTS

CHAPTER I

CHAPTER II

xiii

CHAPTER III

JOURNEY TO ITAHUA

CHAPTER IV

EXPERIENCES IN ZANZIBAR AND FRESH JOURNEY TO
CENTRAL AFRICA

CHAPTER V

FROM UGALLA TO THE KINGDOM OF LUNDA

CHAPTER VI

ENTRY INTO URUA

CHAPTER VII

THE NEW SULTAN OF UTETERA

CHAPTER VIII

THE ARAB TOWNS OF NYANGWE AND KASSONGO

CHAPTER IX

WITH STANLEY DOWN THE CONGO

CHAPTER X

BY TABORA BACK TO ZANZIBAR

CHAPTER XI

FRESH JOURNEY TO STANLEY FALLS

CHAPTER XII

RETURN HOME

CHAPTER XIII

THE FIGHTING ROUND STANLEY FALLS

CHAPTER XIV

CHAPTER XV

CHAPTER XVI

COLLAPSE OF THE ARAB POWER

TIPPOO TIB

CHAPTER I

HISTORICAL INTRODUCTION : EAST AFRICA UP TO THE
REIGN OF SEYYID SAID (1806-1856)

' Marche toujours : un monde est là.'—GUILLAIN.

WHEN, about the middle of the last century, the
attention of a wider circle was directed to the
quarter which people were accustomed to call the
Dark Continent, probably very few of those who
heard of the astounding discoveries of European
travellers—of snowy mountains and vast lakes at
the Equator—realized that thousands of years ago
daring navigators had directed their course to that
very East Coast which in our day was to be the
starting-point of the assault on the secrets of the new
region. No less an authority than the father of
history, Herodotus, informs us that even in primeval
times Phœnician fishermen circumnavigated the
southern extremity of Africa. True, those accounts
are confused, and what they relate is not always to
be reconciled with the geographical knowledge of
our days ; yet as every echo is the reverberation of a
real voice, so there is no fable so foolish but some

1

grain of truth is contained in it. And the mighty ruins of Mashonaland, discovered a few decades ago, and recently more thoroughly explored by Carl Peters, do indeed tell in forcible language of primeval civilization on the East Coast of Africa. We may take it that the Phœnicians and Assyrians, those pioneers of maritime commerce, sowed and reaped here ; and even the mysterious land of Ophir, to which, according to the Old Testament narrative, King Hiram sent his ocean-going ships,* seems to assume palpable form. But over it all floats the veil of the fabulous, which the inquirer may here and there softly lift, but which he can never quite tear away from the stony countenance of the Sphinx, that inexorable guardian of primeval secrets.

In all this chaos of legends and fables only this fact remains established—that these regions were known to the oldest seafaring peoples, just as these knew the Indian Peninsula as long ago as two thousand years before Christ. One of the oldest historical documents we possess concerning the geography of East Africa is the 'Periplus of the Erythræan Sea,'† which appeared at the beginning of our era, and is probably wrongly ascribed to Arrian of Nicodemia (who lived early in the 2nd century), which tells of a great city called Raphta, whose site can indeed be no longer determined, but which in the opinion of most commentators must have

---

* 1 Kings ix., x.

† Compare also for what follows Guillain, 'Documents sur l'Histoire, la Géographie et la Commerce de l'Afrique Orientale' (Paris, 1856), vol. i., p. 81, and Strandes, 'Portugesienzeit in Deutsch- und Englisch-Ostaforka' (Berlin, 1899), p. 81 *et seq.*

lain between the present coast towns of Mombasa
and Mozambique. A later proof of the connection
of East Africa with the Arabian Peninsula is furnished by the fact that in the South Arabian
religious wars of the eighth century negro slaves
formed a considerable portion of the armies engaged.* Their number and power increased so
much that a hundred years later they were able to
enter on a conflict with their oppressors. In 869
a fierce servile war broke out, which, starting from
Bâsra, devastated South Irak and Kurdistan for
fourteen years, and threatened to overthrow the
Arab domination there. The leader of the rebels
was the Arab Ali bin Muhammed, nicknamed El
Khabith (the Monster). His hordes were called the
Zeng, a word equivalent to the Zingis of the Greeks,
which was used to designate the East Coast and its
inhabitants, and which still survives in the word
Zanzibar (Arabic *Zengibar* = Land of the Zeng).

While, then, we have such clear proof that
African natives were carried off in masses as slaves
to more northerly countries, on the other hand,
political conditions in these regions in the seventh
and following centuries were such as could not
fail to favour migration to the new regions. In
630 Muhammed had imposed his doctrines and
political influence on the city of Mecca, from which
he had had to flee eight years before ; two years
later all Arabia lay at his feet. Under his suc-
cessors — Abu Bekr, Omar, and Othman — Islam
began that brilliant career of victory which ended

* Müller, ' Der Islam in Morgen- und Abendland,' Berlin,
1885, vol. i., p. 583 *et seq.*

with the subjugation of Southern Persia, Syria, Egypt, and the whole of North Africa. The assassination of Othman in the year 656 gave the first blow* to the creed which had till then seemed invincible, and sowed the first seed of a fratricidal quarrel which has lasted ever since. Othman's behaviour had shown him to be an unworthy successor of the Prophet, and he fell by the dagger of fanatics. Ali, the cousin and son-in-law of the Prophet, was legally chosen as his successor, but was not recognised by Othman's adherents, who accused him of complicity in the murder of Othman. Moawija was hoisted on the shield by them. Several sanguinary battles were followed in 657 by an armistice, and it was decided to refer to a court of arbitration the question who should be Khalif. But not only was no agreement arrived at : the hoped-for remedy itself proved a source of fresh discord. The very acceptance of the armistice was a sin against the Koran, which forbids making terms with rebels against God's will, and enjoins war to the knife against them. All who implicitly followed the divine precepts separated from the adherents of Ali, and under the name of Kharigites, or Separatists, took up the struggle with those who had rebelled against God's word. In the famous Battle of Nahrawan (658) they were slain almost to a man, but their belief did not perish with them. In 661 a Kharigite murdered Ali, whose son gave up his claims to Moawija, and he in turn became

* Sachau, ' Religiöse Anschauungen der Ibaditischen Muha. medaner,' in the *Mitteilungen des Semmais für Orientalische Sprachen*, Berlin, 1898.

the object of a desperate feud on the part of the Kharigites, which was fatal to the latter. Yet, despite these reverses, the sect survived, and founded a new State in Oman, whose inhabitants were later to be the lords of East Africa ; and such, with their old inflexible religion, they have in a certain sense remained to the present day, greatly as the last decades have undermined their domination.

It is in accordance with human nature that internal dissensions such as those described above should favour migration to peaceful regions. That such actually took place to the East Coast one or two centuries later is established by an old Arab chronicle, which fell into the hands of the Portuguese at the taking of Kilwa in 1505.

This chronicle lays no claim to accuracy, especially in its earlier parts. It sets forth that the first Arab settlers in East Africa were followers of Said, a son of Hussein, the great-grandson of the Prophet. In it they are designated by the Arabic expression ' ummet Said,' which has been corrupted by later writers into ' Emosaides.' These Emosaides are said to have founded no permanent towns, but merely to have lived together for mutual protection. It was not till a century later, apparently, that the first Muhammedan towns were founded, and the first step thus taken towards subjecting the littoral. About A.D. 900, the chronicle relates, a band of Arabs, driven out by the state of affairs at home, fled from the town of El Hasa, on the Persian Gulf, and in three ships, under the leadership of nine brothers, reached the Somali coast, where they founded the towns of Mogdishu and Brawa. A

further migration — a Persian one this time—
followed, according to the chronicle, some seventy
years later. It seems that Ali, a son of Sultan
Hassan, of Persia, left his home in Shiraz owing to
family dissensions. Attracted by stories of the gold
which abounded in Africa, he sailed from Ormuz
with two ships for the settlements mentioned ; but
as he could not get on with the Arabs, he went
further south, and founded the city of Kilwa, which
later attained to great prosperity. A second chronicle
of Kilwa that has come down to us also ascribes the
founding of the city to Ali, although it varies in
details from the version of the first chronicle.
According to the first of the two chronicles Ali's
son Muhammed subsequently founded Mombasa, a
statement confirmed by a still extant chronicle of
the latter city—at least, in so far that, according to
it, the oldest rulers of the city were sheikhs from
Shiraz.

The people to-day still preserve the memory of
an earlier Persian immigration ; and from many
details, into which this is not the place to enter, it
may be taken for certain that for a long time Shirazi
families, with a culture far in advance of the present
Arab civilization, ruled the East Coast, without
driving away by their presence the Arabs previously
settled there, who probably were always numerically
superior to them. A trace of such coexistence of
Arab and Shirazi domination continued in Zanzibar
until lately. The island had long been in possession of the Arabs, and when Said, Sultan of Maskat,
transferred his capital thither in 1832, could be
regarded as a wholly Arab country. Nevertheless,

there reigned side by side with this Sultan, scarcely three hours' journey from his capital, perfectly undisturbed, and without a sign of dependence, under the designation of *Mwinyi Mkuu* (Great Lord), a ruler of undoubted Shirazi descent, whom the original inhabitants of the islands, the Wahadimu and Watambatu, regarded as their legitimate sovereign. This extraordinary state of things did not cease till the death, in 1856, of the last scion of that family. His grave lies close before the palace of the Arab Sultan (in the grounds of the German club). How matters developed further on the East Coast cannot be ascertained from the existing chronicles. After the manner of all Arab records, they give long-winded genealogical tables, which have no interest for posterity, and from which the student can gather but little as to the degree of civilization prevailing at various times. All that need be dwelt on is that towards the end of the twelfth century there appears to have been at Kilwa a ruler of the name of Hassan, who, during a reign of eighteen years, brought his city to a high state of prosperity, and made it the mistress of trade as far down as Sofala. He is said also to have erected a large fortress and many stone buildings.

Mogdishu also must at that time have been an important town, as may be gathered from two inscriptions, dated respectively 1238 and 1269, preserved there. This tallies with other accounts, according to which trade in India, as in the whole Arabian Sea, was at that time particularly flourishing. Even the Chinese, who had long carried on a brisk traffic with India, came to East Africa soon after.

Marco Polo (1270-1293) informs us that the Emperor
of China sent a whole Chinese fleet on a voyage of
discovery to Madagascar, and from later Chinese
sources it appears that Chinese junks visited Mogdishu. The connection of this ancient civilized
nation with our coast is confirmed by the finding of
Chinese coins at Kilwa and Mogdishu. The coins
range from the sixth to the twelfth centuries of
our era.

A new epoch was inaugurated for East Africa
with the voyages of discovery of the Portuguese,
beginning with the circumnavigation of the southern
extremity of the continent by Bartholomeu Dias
(1487) and the voyage to India of Vasco da Gama
(1497-1502). From that time on these lands are
brought geographically nearer to us. In what stage
the Portuguese then found Semitic culture on the
East Coast, whether just at its acme or already
beginning to decline, can hardly be determined;
at any rate, their narratives are full of wonder
at what they saw, which certainly must have
been very different from what they were accustomed to see on the uncivilized West Coast. Along
the whole coast, from Sofala to India, an extensive
traffic was carried on, especially in gold and clothing
material of all kinds. The inhabitants were white
and black Moors (Arabs and Swahili); both races
were well clad and richly decked with gold and
jewels. Soon, by conquest or treachery, the whole
coast became a Portuguese possession. But as yet
only the coast is spoken of. There is no talk of
further penetration into the interior—nay, nothing
appears to be known of the country beyond

the walls of the fortified coast settlements. They content themselves with sucking the goodness out of the country from there. The Portuguese were far worse colonists than the Arabs. Their rule bore within it the seed of death, and two hundred years later no trace of Portuguese conquest remained on African soil. They left nothing distinctive behind them in the country; the towns which they found prospering are in ruins, and only here and there a stone inscription or a cannon buried in the sand of the shore reminds us that centuries ago the long-vanished might of a European nation was displayed here.

After the common enemy had been finally driven away there arose, in the second half of the eighteenth century, an internecine strife between the two Arab races, which again brought serious calamity on the country and ended in the final victory of the Busaid dynasty, the rulers of that Oman already spoken of, a small and wretched little country in the north-east corner of Arabia. Under Sultan Said (1804-1856) a new period of prosperity set in for East Africa. As a lad of sixteen this talented and unscrupulous ruler deposed his uncle, Kis bin Ahmed, from the throne of Oman; a few years later his last enemies in Mombasa had been overthrown by cunning or by force of arms, and when at length, in 1832, he transferred his capital to Zanzibar, a vast realm extending from the north-east extremity of Arabia right down the east coast as far as Cape Delgado was united under his sceptre.

True, here again it is only the coasts of the East African mainland on which a direct political influence

is exercised, but individual attempts to penetrate into
the interior and secure its treasures have already
begun. The gold of Sofala has fallen into oblivion,
but new objects of value have taken its place.
The cultivation of cloves, which had become familiar
in Mauritius, has been introduced in Zanzibar, and
in an astonishingly short time conquers that island
and Pemba, to which it still gives its stamp. Now,
for the working of the clove plantations labour is
needed, and this is furnished in ample measure by
the dark interior. Such of it as cannot be utilized
in the broad plantations is exported, as was the case
over a thousand years before, to the North, to Arabia
and the countries on the Persian Gulf, and brings
rich profits to the slave-hunters and middlemen, and
not less to the ruler of the country, who levies
a considerable poll-tax on every slave brought to
Zanzibar.

A further important article of commerce is ivory,
the thirst for which entices men further and further
into regions where the value of the precious tusk is
not yet known, and for a piece of bright-coloured stuff
any amount can be obtained in exchange from the
inexperienced natives, unless the trader prefers to
take it from them by force. Gradually, too, folks
find their way to the great lakes. On the route to
Tanganyika the town of Tabora has become an
entrepôt, where a great number of Arabs and Indian
traders have taken up their abode, and are ruled by
the Vali, the Sultan's own representative, who ad-
ministers justice there in the name of his master
and is dependent on his commands. On the lake
itself flourishes the town of Ujiji, which again

is subject to the Sultan. In short, a new life has awoke ; trade reaches a high pitch of prosperity, and whoever has the daring necessary to face a journey into the interior, with its dangers, can, in a short space of time, become a rich man.

CHAPTER II

'What from thy fathers thou inherit'st
That earn and make indeed thine own.'
GOETHE : *Faust.*

THE commencement of the journeys undertaken by
daring slave- and ivory-hunters, which led to the
ultimate founding of Tabora and Ujiji, dates back
to a far earlier period, of course, than the reign of
Said just described. The first adventurers must
have found what they sought—viz., slaves and ivory
—in the neighbourhood of the coast. After the
nearer districts had been depopulated or the survivors grown too strong for violence and too artful
in trading, they gradually advanced further and
further ; and he who was brave enough to push forward into unknown tracts always found in the
boundless interior a new sphere to which no Arab
had penetrated before him, and which he, as the first
comer, could exploit. If the inhabitants were warlike and he could not rely on his own strength—a
certain display of force was always an essential in
untried regions—the traveller could resort to the
way of diplomatic manœuvring in peaceful trade and

12

wheedle out of the inexperienced savages the precious ivory, whose value they did not know, at a cheap rate, and could also barter a few pieces of coloured cloth for a whole herd of slaves. If, on the contrary, the natives were weak and victory seemed certain, a shorter procedure was adopted. Peaceful hamlets were surprised and plundered, and such of the natives as could be captured were carried off as slaves. In this fashion many an Arab who went forth a poor man must have returned home wealthy, and there by the tales he told or the display of his wealth spread the news that in East Africa, with a little audacity, a man might soon become rich. The success of the first comers constantly incited fresh adventurers to seek fortune in these unknown regions.

It was this spirit of adventure that about the middle of the last century led a member of a respected Muscat family, Juma bin Muhammed el Nebhani, to the gainful coast of East Africa. He settled at Mbwa Maji, a small village to the south of the present German capital of Dar-es-Salaam. There he married a negress, who bore him three children—a son named Muhammed and two daughters, the eldest called Mwana Arabu. Having grown rich, he returned to his home at Muscat with his son, who had meanwhile grown up, to end his days there. His son, however, went back to East Africa, this time in company with Rajab bin Muhammed bin Said el Murgebi, the great-grandfather of our hero. To him he gave in marriage his sister Mwana Arabu, who had remained behind at Mbwa Maji, and from this union sprang Juma bin Rajab, an enterprising leader of caravans, who, by daring raids to Tabora and Lake Tanganyika, was already winning great influence.

Through him Mwura, grandfather of the afterwards so much dreaded bandit Mirambo, became Sultan of Ujoa, a small tract lying west of Uriakuru. Later on he travelled together with his son Muhammed, Tippoo Tib's father, who raised himself still further by an advantageous marriage. Fundi Kira, the then powerful Sultan of Tabora, gave him his daughter Karunde to wife. But as the Muhammedan is allowed to have four wives—the number of concubines whom he may choose as well from among his slaves is unlimited, and depends entirely on the means of the individual—he married besides at Zanzibar the daughter of a respected and prosperous Muscat family, Bint Habib bin Bushir, of the clan of Wardi, who had previously been married to her relative Masud bin Muhammed, but had been divorced by him—a common occurrence among Arabs.

From this new marriage sprang Hamed bin Muhammed, surnamed Tippoo Tib. He first saw the light at the *shamba* of Kwarara, in Zanzibar, belonging to a relative of his mother's. His bringing-up was, in accordance with Arab custom, the simplest conceivable. At about six years of age he was handed over to an ignorant tutor to learn reading and writing by the help of the Koran. After the attempt had failed in the case of the first teacher, he was entrusted to a second, who, when the usual period of learning was at an end, dismissed him as an 'educated man.' As he grew up he made

himself as useful as he could on his mother's
property; at sixteen he set out on his first journey.
Together with some relatives on his mother's side,
among them his half-brother Bushir bin Habib,
he travelled the opposite coast, trading in copal,
at first on a small scale, as suited his slender
credit.

At eighteen he was summoned by his father, who
usually lived at Tabora, but came now and again to
the coast, to undertake a great journey. At Ugangi,
north-east of Lake Nyassa, they traded in ivory and
slaves, selling their acquisitions later on at Zanzibar.
When the father returned to Tabora he took his son
with him. On the way the latter was attacked by
the small-pox, a disease which never quite dies out
in East Africa, and has left its cruel mark on many
a negro and Arab face. Thus the unhappy pretender
to the throne, Seyyid Khalid, son of the powerful Sultan Burghash, who lives at Dar-es-salaam, has
had his fine Oriental features woefully disfigured by
it. The disease, strange to say, has left no visible
traces on Tippoo Tib; his beauty would have suffered no loss even if it had, for, apart from the
negative advantage of having no pock-marks, Tippoo
Tib can certainly not claim to be an Adonis. His
face shows the thorough negro type, which is the
more remarkable as he comes of a good Arab family,
and his pedigree was only defaced by his grand-
mother on the father's side, who was a negress.
None the less, he may call himself an Arab, for folks
only ask about the origin of the father. The child
of the blackest slave-woman counts for as much as
the offspring of a princess if it is only born in

legitimate wedlock.   And, in spite of its easy disso-
lution, every matrimonial alliance of a Muhammedan
with any of his female slaves is legitimate.

But to return to our chronological narrative.   In
Unyanyembe, the country of Tippoo Tib's father,
a stay of only two months was made; then the
party went on, accompanied by a goodly band of
Arabs, to Ujiji, on Lake Tanganyika.   Here, however, they found the prices of ivory unfavourable,
so most of the Arabs determined to try their luck
on the west side of Tanganyika, in Urua.   Old
Muhammed was recalled to Tabora by his duties as
ruler, so he commissioned his son to trade for him
in the new country, taking with him the objects of
barter that were current there—pearls and mussels.
But he was to travel under the supervision of an
experienced man of the coast.   Here the independent
temper of the young merchant showed itself for the
first time.   Though hardly eighteen, he indignantly
rejected the suggestion that he should carry on his
business under the control of another.   'If you want
to trust your wares to this Swahili, and I am to be
under him, it is better I should go back with you.'
The old man put it to him that he was still young
and did not know trade in Urua; gladly as he
would have entrusted the guidance of the caravan
to him, he (Tippoo Tib) must really give way
this time.   But Tippoo Tib remained obdurate,
declaring that he must try it for once; if things
went wrong, in future his father might trust his
affairs to whom he pleased.   He thus obtained his
father's permission, and set out on his journey.   In
great canoes—the hollowed-out trunks of mighty

trees, such as only the primeval forest produces—
they crossed Tanganyika in primitive fashion.

It was a numerous band which took the way
towards the little-known West : not less than twenty
Arabs were eager to open up fresh sources of profit
in the new country. They reached the abode of
Mwagu Tambu, a Sultan of friendly disposition.
The traffic in ivory was not exceptional, but it was
tolerable. Large tusks were dear, small ones comparatively cheap. While the other Arabs purchased
the dearer large tusks, Tippoo Tib decided to buy
the smaller specimens, and in doing so made a
lucky speculation, as was shown later on the coast.

As a rule large tusks, be it said, are more ex-
pensive, and of these, again, the soft ones, as being
easier to work, are from 20 to 30 per cent. dearer
than the hard ones.* Among the soft tusks the
following distinctions are made : Large tusks of
best quality and slightly curved, suitable for making
billiard-balls, have been quoted of late years at
from 114 to 145 dollars (£17 to £23) per *frasila*
(35 pounds). The next best kind, which is particularly suitable for piano keys, is called, because it
is principally exported to Europe, ' Bab Ulaia,' and
of late years has fetched from 105 to 130 dollars
(£15 to £20) per *frasila*. A third kind is exported
to India, and is therefore called ' Bab Cutch,' and is
used for the making of arm and leg rings. It fetches
from 95 to 113 dollars (£14 to £17). Small tusks,
which are obtained from the younger elephants, are

---

* *Cf.* the Trade Reports for at home and abroad, sepa-
rately published by the German Ministry of the Interior,
Series III., No. 1, December, 1899.

relatively much cheaper, yet they may also, under
certain circumstances, reach high prices. As they
are often used as ornaments when mounted in silver,
the attractiveness of their shape and the fancy of
the purchaser are the chief factors in determining
their price. It is thus quite intelligible that Tippoo
Tib was lucky in his speculation in small tusks; he
would have been even more successful with them
to-day, as in order to spare the breed of elephants,
both the German and the British Governments have
forbidden the shooting of young elephants.

After finishing their business they came on the
way back to Mtoa, on the western shore of Tanganyika. Here they heard of great changes that had
taken place meanwhile in their new home, Unyanyembe. Fundikira, the Sultan of Tabora, was dead,
and the Overlord of the country had set up his
nephew, Mnywa Sere (the 'Tembo-drinker'), as his
successor. This aggrieved another relative, Mkasiva,
who, being nearer to the throne, made preparations
to wrest from the other his usurped sovereignty.
Mnywa Sere did not wait to be attacked, but tried to
crush his opponent before he grew too strong. A
twenty days' conflict, however, resulted indecisively.
He then turned for help to old Muhammed, whom
he induced by rich presents of ivory to support him
with a great number of Arabs and their dependents.
Within a month Mkasiva was decisively routed, a
great portion of his followers killed, and others taken
prisoners, while he himself escaped with difficulty
to Uriankuru.

This cheaply-earned victory went to the 'Tembo-
drinker's' head, so that he began to oppress his

former helpers, primarily in the shape of 'hongo'
or toll, an institution to which the chiefs in the interior, when they were strong enough, always resorted
to enrich themselves at the expense of passing
caravans. Where there was no help for it, people put
up with this, only the contribution had to be kept
within reasonable bounds. With Mnywa Sere this
was not the case : he made very large demands, and
the business was highly profitable, for the immigration of Arabs was about this time particularly great,
favoured by the political events in Zanzibar, which
drove a great number of them to leave their homes.
In 1856 Seyyid* Said, the powerful Sultan, had
died ; he was the last of his race to unite the
dominions in East Africa and Oman under one
sceptre. A great lover of women, he had owned a
splendid harem, from which had sprung some
twenty sons, beside numerous daughters. The eldest,
Thueni, took the reins in Oman ; in Zanzibar Majid
ascended the throne, much to the grief of his next
brother, afterwards Sultan Burghash, who would
have liked to become ruler himself. After various
smaller intrigues, he made in 1859 a determined
attempt to overthrow Seyyid Majid.

In the interior of the island, some four hours'
journey from the city, lies a country-seat, to which
Said, who was greatly under French influence,
had given the name of Marseille. Now that the

---

* 'Seyyid' signifies 'lord,' and is the attribute of the Sultan
and his belongings. 'Said,' with a guttural sound before the ι,
is a proper name, and means 'lucky.' In Swahili pronunciation
the two words sound almost alike, and so they are mostly
wrongly reproduced by European writers.

importance of France in Zanzibar has diminished
people have forgotten the foreign title, and gone
back to the old name Machui, which signifies something like 'in the wilderness.' Here Burghash
had assembled his forces, after an attempt in the city
had failed. Majid, who was too weak to contend
with Burghash alone, called to his aid the English,
who placed a detachment of sailors at his disposal.
An inglorious attack, in which the Sultan's troops
and the English contended for the lead—the wrong
way about—failed indeed, yet so far alarmed Burghash that he stole away in the night and concluded peace. He was exiled to Bombay, and his
adherents were likewise banished or imprisoned,
those that were well-to-do being further punished
with confiscations of property, an arrangement as
painful to the sufferer as gratifying to the inflicter.
Greatly injured in this way, and still not secure
against Majid's vengeance, many Arabs migrated,
to seek a new home in the interior, chiefly at
Tabora and on Tanganyika. Descendants of the
fugitives of that day are still numerous at Tabora.

To these haughty Arabs it was, of course, mon-
strous to endure the oppression of a 'Shensi'—
a savage—and so the bitterness against Mnywa
Sere grew more and more; yet no one dared undertake anything against the favourite of old Muhammed.
At length the tyrant himself made the measure run
over by daring to have Karunde's uncle and mother
murdered. If Muhammed had been a Western and
a reader of 'Fliegende Blätter,' he might, perhaps,
have regarded the doing away with his mother-in-law
as a friendly action; but, being an Oriental, he fell

into a passion over this interference in his family
affairs, and planned revenge. He was at Ituru—
the settlement belonging to him in the immediate
neighbourhood of Tabora—when he learnt the news
of the outrage. The Arabs living there were only
too ready to follow him in arms. 'We have long
been inclined,' they declared, ' to strike the tyrant ; it
is only out of consideration for you that we have put
up with his oppressions.' Immediately the plan of
action was framed. It was proposed to band together
all the Arabs resident in the district, to wait for the
coming of Tippoo Tib and his companions, which
was expected shortly, and in the meantime to send
secretly to Mkasiva, whom it was proposed to
draw out of concealment, and set up as the successor of Mnywa Sere. This last mission was undertaken by the Arab Salum bin Sef el Bahari. In
the remaining preparations the most prominent
was taken by Thenei bin Amur, a ' Besar '—*i.e.*,
an Arab from Oman, only not of pure blood, but
the issue of the slave caste. These ' Besars ' as a
rule occupy a subordinate position socially as compared with the full-blooded Arabs, the ' Kubails,'
whom they have to address as ' Hebabi,' or ' Lord ' ;
but often they are far superior to them in intelligence, and attain to considerable wealth — an
advantage which, as money everywhere is in
good repute, in its turn helps to raise their importance. Thenei was one of these honourable
exceptions to his class, and enjoyed great consideration among the Arabs. His proposal that all
Arabs should assemble at one place, and thus stand
prepared for a possible sudden attack by Mnywa

Sere, was readily adopted, the more so as he
closed his instructions with the pithy comment :
'He who does not hearken to me understands
nothing of the conduct of war ; let him hereafter,
if things go wrong, blame not me, but himself'
(from the Koran : Sura Ibrahim, xiv. 27).

The place of assembly appointed was the hamlet
of Kwihara, not far from Tabora, where within
twelve days some 300 to 400 Arabs with their
attendants were gathered. Tippoo Tib with his
men also arrived at this stage of the preparations,
and took up his quarters with Sultan bin Ali,
the chief of Kwihara. The latter had as yet no
idea of the plan of campaign, and may well have
been astonished to find such a number of guests
on his hands. With true Arab hospitality, however,
he set his best before them; for, according to custom,
the host may not ask till the third day what brings
the stranger to him. But presumably they initiated
him before that.

It all but went ill with them as they were feasting
at Kwihara, for Mnywa Sere had got wind of their
intentions, and endeavoured to frustrate them by
attacking first. There lived at Tabora an Indian
trader, Musa, surnamed the Handsome, who some
years before, following the migration westward, had
come to the country, in company with a compatriot
who had since died, to promote civilization by the
sale of brandy and other modern requirements.
One of his principal customers was Mnywa Sere,
who bartered the to him valueless ivory with the
ingenious middleman for the marvels of European
and Indian industry.

At this time messengers from the Sultan had just come on matters of business to the Indian. As his interest required, the handsome Musa at once gave these people the necessary hints. 'The Arabs are planning something against your Sultan. They have assembled at Kwihara, at Sultan bin Ali's, and are only waiting for Mkasiva, whom they mean to set up as the new Sultan.' In all haste the messengers conveyed the weighty news to their master, who in his first eagerness formed the sensible resolution to be the first in the field, and by an immediate attack on the Arabs loitering at Kwihara put a speedy end to the war; but, with the usual recklessness of the negro, in the end he allowed himself to be persuaded by his indolent followers to wait till he was attacked. 'One could not tell as yet whether the whole thing was not a fraud. And even if it was true, he would by-and-by make child's play of conquering the Arabs.' He had at that time, Tippoo Tib declares, a large force. 'If he had come it would have been most dangerous for us, and our food would probably have never tasted sweet to us again.'

At length Mkasiva arrived. The war for which such ample preparations had been made began. For three months they ravaged, burned, and plundered ; and then the power of the 'Tembo-drinker' was broken. He himself escaped, and Mkasiva became Sultan. Soon after the war Tippoo Tib returned to the coast.

CHAPTER III

JOURNEY TO ITAHUA

'He ever was a wicked wight;
Him Heaven's vengeance smote aright.'
F. KIND : *Freischütz*.

AT Zanzibar Tippoo Tib first carried out certain
commissions of his father's : he sold his ivory and
sent him further articles of barter in the interior.
He himself did not for the present return to Un-
yanzembe, but began to travel on his own account.
As he naturally, as a young beginner, had but scanty
credit—he had to borrow money in sums of from
one to a thousand dollars—he contented himself for
the time with smaller undertakings ; but as he succeeded in these he extended his expeditions further
into the interior, and at last undertook a longer
journey into the Tanganyika districts, which
brought him in much ivory and probably many
slaves as well. When he returned from this tour
to Zanzibar, twelve years had passed since his first
trip to Tabora. In that time he had become a rich
man.

Things had not gone so well with his young half-
brother and friend, Muhammed bin Masud el Wardi,
whom now for the first time he saw again in their

24

home after a long separation. In the meantime
he had tried his luck in another way. He had
'traded,' as it is very discreetly styled in Tippoo
Tib's jottings, between Ngao, the southern coast
district of our colony, and the Benadir coast.
On my asking further the nature of this trading,
Tippoo Tib had to own with a smirk that his
brother had undertaken slave-hunts in the south,
and sold his booty in more northerly regions. He
had not grown rich from it, for his friend Muhammed bin Said el Herthi, with whom he had been
in partnership in the business, had recklessly
squandered all the takings, and left nothing over
for him. He therefore gladly joined his brother,
who was already beginning to be famous, when the
latter again started for the interior. To be sure,
he could contribute as yet only on a small scale, for
it was not possible for him to borrow more than
5,000 dollars.

Tippoo Tib, on the other hand, started with goods
to the value of 30,000 dollars, though he had to
search diligently for people who would give him
credit. He left twenty creditors behind oscillating
between fear and hope. It was no light matter, in
view of the uncertain conditions, to stake much
money on a caravan for the interior. How many
of them never came back again! Either the whole
was wiped out by savages or the leader died, and
all the property was made away with by his unskilful or faithless followers. In many cases, too,
the debtor preferred, instead of abiding by his
obligations in Zanzibar, to lead a showy life in the
interior with other people's money. Wissmann, in

his crossing of Africa in 1883, encountered such a worthy * in Nyangwe. On the other hand, the profit was all the greater when a debtor came back richly laden from the interior. The Indians keep a good tally; they are not apt to forget anything; indeed, they are more likely to enter an item twice over to make sure. And the Arab, to whom book-keeping is an abomination—the acknowledgment of a debt is the only document he ever keeps —pays willingly, provided he has the means, in order to keep up his credit. He will need the cashbox of his Indian business friend for his next expedition. Of those who enter into such speculations, the Swahili say, ' Wanabahatisha sana ' ('They tempt Fortune ').

So the journey began, and not under very favourable auspices. On the mainland there was a famine. In order not to pass through quite impoverished districts, Tippoo Tib chose, instead of the ordinary route by Usagara and Ugogo, the more southerly one by Urori, which also, as being little used, was the richer in ivory. But the Wanyamwezi — the tribe that usually furnishes the carriers (and very good ones)—declined to follow him there. The negro is in the highest degree conservative. What runs counter to *dasturi*, or ancient custom, is distasteful to him. The Wanyamwezi had been used in former journeys always to pass through Usagara and then through their native country, and now all of a sudden it

* Abed bin Salem. *Cf.* Wissmann, ' Unter Deutscher Flagge quer durch Afrika,' Berlin, 1889, pp. 181, 182.

was to be through Urori, a quite unknown region.
They were not going to agree to that !

Then—a blessing in disguise—the famine came
to the rescue in the difficulty. The Wasaramo, a
tribe which usually would not condescend to porter's
work, found themselves compelled by hard times
to adopt that profitable means of livelihood. Two
hundred men were speedily enlisted, and they were
not dear. In addition to their keep, they got for
the whole journey, which would probably last whole
years, 10 dollars—*i.e.*, at the present rate, about
30 marks. From a fourth to a third of this was
given to them beforehand. The journey began from
Mbwa Maji, the place already mentioned, on the
coast south of Dar-es-Salaam, at first in a southerly
direction towards Rufiji. They crossed the little
river Mbezi, and in three days reached Mkamba,
where a halt was called, that they might equip
themselves for a six days' journey through districts
devoid of food.

When the drum of the caravan sounded on the
day appointed for the start, an unpleasant surprise
was in store, which has brought many an African
traveller to despair. The porters, delighted with
their advance and in happy possession of provisions
for six days, had made off in a body. The *ngoma*
might resound as loudly as it would, not a carrier
appeared. The men who were sent to the various
quarters of the Wasaramo—of course, the whole
700 had not found shelter in one place, but had
housed themselves in the neighbouring villages,
sixty men to a village—returned, unsuccessful ; no
one came. 'Then my reason deserted me,' writes

Tippoo Tib himself. He seems, however, to have been still capable of sound deliberation, for he at once called out his men, and proceeded with eighty guns back along the way he had come. They marched till dark, then simply bivouacked on the high-road, and the next morning reached the first abodes of the Wasaramo.

The fugitives had, it is true, not yet arrived, but what did that matter to the Arab sense of justice? The whole tribe had to pay for the misdeeds of its sons. Quickly enough 200 people were seized and put in irons. Resistance to the armed Swahilis was not to be thought of. So they moved, plundering and burning, from place to place, and within five days 800 people had been taken captive. The promptness with which Tippoo Tib had acted earned him the title of 'Kingugwa chui'—*i.e.*, the 'Leopard,' who breaks in now here, now there.

On being seized, they were temporarily secured in wooden yokes, such as every slave-hunter used, and taken to Mkamba, where an Indian merchant, Banyane Hila, lived. From him Tippoo Tib procured iron rods and had chains forged of them by workmen whom he had taken with him expressly for that purpose. In these he put the involuntary carriers, and with them finally began his march. To ensure that no one should escape, he himself brought up the rear ; at the head marched his brother, Muhammed bin Masud, whose powerful military following earned him among the Shensis the name of 'Kumbakumba,' 'the Gatherer of Everything.'

Thus they reached Urori, where the powerful

Sultan Merere was then reigning. He had formerly
been friendly to the Arabs, but later, being incensed
at the wanton acts of travellers, changed his policy
and attacked various caravans of his former friends.
A certain Amran bin Masud, one of the Arabs who
had fled after the unsuccessful attempt of Burghash,
had avenged his compatriots on him, and so far
humbled him that he was willing to purchase peace
by a yearly payment of a hundred tusks.   The
victor would not agree to this.   Later the fortune of
war changed : Amran himself was defeated and lost
his life in the conflict.

When Tippoo Tib came there the country had
just been reopened to peaceful traffic, and the conditions of trade were the most favourable conceivable.   For from twelve to fifteen garments a *frasila*
of ivory was to be had.   It could be purchased
also for a *frasila* of spices or a chest of soap,
or for 15 pounds of powder.   This happy state of
trade caused Tippoo Tib to leave one of his men
behind in the country, to carry on business on his
account, to whom he entrusted goods to the value
of 6,000 dollars.   He himself proceeded with the
bulk of the caravan to Ruemba, where he was
amicably received by the Sultan, but was unable to
make any profitable bargains.   This was mostly the
case.   Where the Arabs were wanted they were
well received, but there was nothing profitable to
be gained by them.

Then Tippoo Tib resolved to go to Itahua, a
country which then bore a very bad reputation.   A
Sultan ruled there named Nsama, a powerful and
most bloodthirsty chief, of whom all Arabs who had

hitherto entered his territory had had a bad experience. Tippoo Tib left his brother Muhammed
bin Masud behind at Ruemba with 15 guns, and
himself marched with 105 guns through Urunga to
the dreaded country. Everywhere on the way the
natives endeavoured to hold him back by tales of
Nsama's power and cruelty. Moreover, an old Arab
named Amer bin Said esh Shaqsi, who had spent
years in the country, frightened him with an
account of an expedition which he had made a considerable time ago with other Arabs, but from
which very few had returned with whole skins.
But our wanderer was powerfully attracted to this
rich country, for all accounts agreed in affirming
that there were untold treasures of ivory there. So
he and his men crossed the stream which forms the
boundary between Urungu and Itahua.

Immediately on entering the country he acquired
an idea of its wealth. They marched through
luxuriant plantations from one populous township
to another, and the natives were immoderately
haughty towards the intruders. This was no
wonder, for only a short time before they had
given proof of their power. The robber tribe of
the Wangoni, a terror to all adjacent countries, had
endeavoured to surprise Nsama's powerful realm as
well, but had been driven off with bloody sconces.
Their defeat had contributed to heighten the repute
of Nsama's invincibility. The neighbouring tribes
had long been tributary to him, Ruemba and
Urungu—nay, even the nearer townships of the
great central African kingdom of Urua paid him
contributions. After six days' march the caravan

reached a mountain, at the foot of which was built
a great city, Nsama's capital. Like all East African
towns in old days, and many even now, it was
strongly fortified with palisades, thorn-hedges and
trenches.* Tippoo Tib pitched his camp outside
the city on a spot assigned to him by Nsama's
people. The next morning he with the other Arabs
was summoned before the Sultan. As to the recep-
tions and the events which followed it, we will
allow him to give his own account.

'We went and took him such and such garments as a present. He was then a very old man,
between eighty-six and ninety. He said to his
attendants : " Carry me, so that I may show them
the ivory." Then he was carried on their shoulders,
and showed us a very great stock of ivory in the
storehouses. Thereupon I said to him : " Sultan,
will you not give us two tusks ?" Then he suddenly
began to abuse me, and we could see that all the
goods we had given the fellow were a dead loss.
To the other Sultans we gave but few goods, and
they used to give us each two or three tusks, while
this man, to whom we had given a large present,
abused me.

'We took our leave and went to our camp. The
next morning he sent us a messenger to summon
us. We were to go into his city ; all Arabs were
sent for. People were to come with us, too, to
carry away the ivory. But he held his soldiers in
readiness in great numbers, and we knew nothing
of it. We went to the number of twenty, and took

* *Cf.* Wissmann, 'Afrika : Schilderungen und Ratschläge.'
Berlin, 1895. Pp. 19 *et seq.*

ten of our slaves with us. When we got there I, who was walking in front, was hit by three arrows— two hit me fairly, the other more slightly. A young man named Said bin Sef el Maamri was also wounded by a well-aimed arrow, and two slaves were wounded by arrows, and died at once. But we had our guns at the ready, loaded with bullets and biggish shot, and they were standing in separate groups. At a shot they fell like birds. When our guns began to crackle 200 people fell at once; others were trampled down, and so died. They hurriedly took to flight. Within an hour over 1,000 fell. On our side only the two slaves and we two were wounded, and the town was really very large. So they were routed and fled. They took their Sultan with them. At last, by two o'clock, there was not a soul left in the city, except blind people and such as had had their noses or arms cut off, for he was very cruel. If one of his people committed any offence, he used to put out his eyes, or cut off his nose or an arm. We took these to our camp, and found our folks uninjured and in good condition, goods and all. Thereupon we went back to the city.

'Towards evening the enemy came in bands and surrounded the city. Some said, " We will break in in the night and slay them "; others, " We will try to break in towards morning." They had come in great masses, even the Sultan's sons, who lived at some distance—all had come except those who lived very far off. But I was wounded by the arrows which had struck me. I called Bushir bin Hahib el Wardi, my uncle, and said to him : " What do you

think about it ? Choose out the best men who are
not afraid." And he got together some fifty or
sixty of the best guns, and gave the men coarse
shot, and they loaded the guns with shot and bullets.
But the others, when they saw themselves so strong,
and found that we were only few men, took courage:
they lighted fires, and beat their drum, and smoked
hemp and tobacco. Then I and Bushir bin
Habib gave orders, and said to them : " Ten guns
are to go to each door, for they will not see us
because of their fire. Then shoot, and when you
have fired off your guns come back." And they
went, ten guns to the appointed door. When they
came near the guns crackled, and on every side
they fired off their charge at once, so that the
Shensis said : " Perhaps they have pulled down the
boma." Then the men came back. Suddenly we
heard the Shensis calling to each other, then they
lay down where they stood.

' The next morning, about a quarter to seven, our
men went out, and saw that about 600 Shensis had
fallen, and the weapons—spears, arrows, bows,
drums, and axes—which they had thrown away
were not to be counted. They had stood in groups,
you see. We waited a short time. When it was
two o'clock the Shensis advanced on us in great
crowds. However, they were already frightened.
We let them come close to the *boma*, then our
people charged ; and not seven minutes had passed
when they took to flight, and 150 men had fallen,
while we had been lucky—only two men fell. And
they were pursued a space of over two hours, then
our people came back. Finally, on the third day

3

even more of them came than on any of the
previous days, and they came quite close to the
boma. Our people charged, and routed the enemy,
over 250 of whom were killed, and they were pursued a long distance. Not till seven hours afterwards did our men come back. On our side only
three men were killed and four wounded.

'After that day they did not come back again,
and there was no one there who claimed the ivory
in the town. And we were in fear, for the country
was large and the inhabitants many. And from
the capital it was a quick four days' march with
loads to Urungu, by the way we had come. And
we remained in the city, in great fear, until I had
recovered from those arrow wounds. When I
was well I called together my men, freeborn
and slaves, and said to them: "What do you
advise me to do?" But no one answered me.
Then I said to them: "I have determined to march
out and look for them, for for many days we have
not known where they lie."

'Then spake Bushir bin Habib el Wardi: "I
will go; it is not good for you to march, for you
are not strong enough yet." And he left twenty
guns behind; he set off with all the rest. Even the
people that had no guns—some 500 men—he took
with him. About seven o'clock they started, and
we waited till about five o'clock, when they had not
yet come back, nor had we heard anything of them.
And we were greatly afraid. At last, towards sunset, we heard the *ngoma* sound from beyond the
mountain, and they fired guns, and gave vent to a
shout of joy. Then they came themselves.'

They brought rich booty with them, some
1,000 slaves, and an untold number of goats. To
be sure, a drop of gall was mingled with the rejoicing.
On the march towards the frontier they had seen
the corpses of many men of the coast that were
unknown to them. As it afterwards turned out, a
great caravan from Urungu had come into Nsama's
country to buy ivory by the same route by which
Tippoo Tib had marched. They came to the
country just when Nsama was defeated. Out of
revenge, the strangers, who no doubt were believed
to be in league with Tippoo Tib, were attacked and
cut down to the last man. The whole of their
merchandise fell a prey to the Shensis. Tippoo Tib
now waited a few days more. But as nothing further
was heard of the enemy, he was able to give himself up to the pleasant conviction that he remained
the final victor.

The first thing was to secure the booty. Of ivory
alone there appeared to be 1,950 *frasilas*, which,
taking the *frasila* at the then price of £7, gave a
profit of £13,650. At the present day, when a
frasila costs about £15, the ivory taken would
produce, in round numbers, £30,000 — a small
fortune. In addition to this, they took 700 *frasilas*
of copper and a quantity of salt.

With these spoils Tippoo Tib returned to Urungu.
He was greatly honoured by the Sultan there,
Chungu, for Chungu had long been an enemy of
Nsama, at whose tardy fall he was naturally delighted. He at once offered to support the Arabs in
further warfare against Nsama. With his help a
deliberate war of extermination was carried on

against Itahua, which, after two months, ended in
Nsama's entire overthrow. He was granted peace
in return for the payment of a large tribute. In
these conflicts Tippoo Tib, who was still suffering
from the effects of his wounds, did not take part,
but remained at Urungu.

Here he also met the English missionary Livingstone, to whose accounts we owe much concerning
these regions and the events of that time. Although
they are written in primitive fashion—the explorer,
who was devoid of all proper means, at times used
the edgings of newspaper sheets and ink from a
tree for his jottings—yet, however fragmentary they
may be, they are certainly accurate, and often more
reliable than the reports of Tippoo Tib, mostly
somewhat boastfully compiled. Moreover, the Arab
never makes a good historian. Whoever reads our
hero's autobiography will feel that he suffers from
the same prolixity as the chronicles cited at the
outset of the oldest African history. Livingstone
was then on his last journey, which he began in the
early part of 1866 from Zanzibar, and on which, in
April, 1873, he found his death in the village of
Itala. He had marched up the Rowuma to the
Nyassa, and had passed through the same districts
as Tippoo Tib. He made the, to us, interesting
discovery that the Arabs had only penetrated to
Urungu a very short time before. The older natives
could still very well remember the time when there
were no Muhammedans in the country, and as
yet the Moslem faith had not spread far.

On May 12, 1867, he heard that the Arabs had
come to blows with Nsama. Accounts varied as to

the reason of the quarrel, and it was difficult to get to the bottom of the matter. The friendly Arabs Said bin Ali bin Mansur and Thani bin Swelim recounted that Nsama's people had gathered in threatening fashion round the Arabs, who in their alarm fired, whereupon Nsama fled and left the assailants behind in the village. Others declared that a dispute had arisen about an elephant's tusk. Both accounts can be reconciled with Tippoo Tib's statement as to the origin of the quarrel. But Livingstone's reports as to the issue of the conflict differ. According to him, the Arabs were by no means sure of success; they daily practised sorceries to discover how the further conflict with Nsama would turn out. So, too, the accounts of the booty obtained must have been exaggerated, for Livingstone received the impression that Tippoo Tib had lost greatly by the Nsama expedition. The Arabs themselves confess to having lost fifty men against him. Nsama seems to have lost only a few more. According to his accounts, too, the Arabs had only 20 guns at their disposal, while Tippoo Tib speaks of 105. Certainly the Livingstonian version would redound more to his credit, for the English explorer characterizes Nsama as the Napoleon of those regions.

On July 29 the two travellers met at Ponda, a village three days' journey from Lake Mueru. According to his journal, Tippoo Tib presented Livingstone with a goat, a piece of white cotton, four large bushels of beads, and a bag of *sorghum*, and begged him to excuse his not being able to give more. Livingstone also records that Tippoo

Tib had received two wounds in the fighting with Nsama.

From Livingstone's very concise notes of the meeting with Tippoo Tib we gather thus much—that the latter met him in a very friendly spirit. The Arab traveller's description of the rencontre is still more in his favour. It appears that he found Livingstone destitute of all supplies. He describes him as quite an old man, and adds that his name was Livingstone, but that in the interior he called himself David. As an Arab, of course, he did not know the difference between Christian name and surname, and therefore regarded the two words as different names, just as he and his companions had their nicknames in the interior. Livingstone thus seems, like some other Europeans nowadays, to have been obliged, for the sake of greater intimacy, to have himself called simply by his Christian name by his blacks. This may bring the European humanly nearer to his inferiors, but in most cases undermines his authority. The black wants to feel a master over him ; he has no respect for a brother.

According to his descriptions, Tippoo Tib all but saved Livingstone from destruction. He supplied him for several days, conducted him to Lake Mueru, and later on sent him with letters of recommendation to Runda to his friend Muhammed bin Saleh, an old Arab, who then took him in hand. Tippoo Tib also declared that he received various chests from Livingstone, together with a request to send them to Ujiji for him ; these he at once forwarded on an opportunity happening to present itself, and that at his own expense. How far these statements

are founded on fact cannot be estimated. On the
one hand, the events lie so far back that a mistake
of Tippoo Tib's, who simply relates from memory,
is not impossible ; on the other hand, Tippoo Tib,
who always likes to play the *grand seigneur*, constantly distinguished himself by chivalrous hospitality. Livingstone, for his part, cannot withhold
his approval from the Arabs in those parts ; he finds
them differing very advantageously from the slave-
hunters whom he was accustomed to encounter in
Ngao.

In addition to this, Tippoo Tib always felt himself attracted to Europeans. At a very early date
he became convinced of the essential inferiority of
his fellow-tribesmen, and may have divined even
then that the Europeans were a superior breed, with
whom would rest the ultimate victory over those
who had hitherto been the rulers of the country. In
Zanzibar Europeans had long been settled, who
had traversed the broad seas and provided Muhammedan countries with treasures of civilization
hitherto undreamt of by the Oriental. And that
political power was combined with this wealth was
proved by the warships of the Christians, which
from time to time appeared in African waters, and
had a wholly different aspect from the vessels of
their Sultan, which seemed so powerful to the
Zanzibaris. And though the English missionary
whom the Arab traveller met here in the interior
presented such a modest and even wretched appearance, yet the Oriental bowed before the spirit of
enterprise which drove forth the man of the West
to pursue with the simplest means ideals un-

known to him, yet assuredly not worthless. What at that time, perhaps, was half instinct became later firm conviction in Tippoo Tib, and, like a born diplomat, he always sided with the Europeans, even against his own countrymen, as soon as it seemed advantageous to him. His later history will furnish several further instances of this.

It is thus not improbable that events may have actually passed as Tippoo Tib relates them. That Livingstone is silent about many occurrences proves nothing in view of the nature of his accounts, which are only quite short entries in a diary, made under the most difficult circumstances. On September 9 he had an interview with Nsama, whom he visited in his new *boma*, built close beside the old. He depicts him as an old man with a good head and face. As he could no longer walk, his people had to carry him. His belly was greatly swollen from much drinking of pombe. He showed himself very friendly towards Livingstone as soon as he had assured himself of his peaceful intentions, and promised to furnish him with guides for subsequent journeys in his territory. The negotiations, how-ever, led to no result, as they were constantly in-terrupted by Nsama's people, who bore themselves very disrespectfully towards their ruler. Nsama seems really to have been very much given to alcohol, for a month later—October 18—Livingstone writes in his diary that the last he had heard of him was that he, a man of eighty, was performing dances to a musical accompaniment played by two women, and so would appear to have fallen into his dotage. In reality, however, it seems to have been only a

question of a passing attack of drunken madness, for
the Arabs maintained friendly relations with him for
a long time afterwards. Only with his conqueror,
Tippoo Tib, Nsama would have nothing more
to do.

It must also be mentioned that it was in these
struggles that our hero received his well-known
name. He himself declares that the Shensis, unac-
customed to the firing of guns, called him so because
his muskets always went ' tip, tip.' Livingstone
writes, on the other hand, that the sheikh, at the
sight of Nsama's treasures, exclaimed : ' Now I am
Tippoo Tib, the gatherer of wealth.' If so, the
etymology of the word remains obscure, for neither
in Arabic nor in Swahili have the words the meaning attached to them by Livingstone. It can only
be that a corresponding expression occurs in the
Itahua language. Another version is also prevalent
as to the origin of the name—viz., that Hamed
bin Muhammed was so called on account of his
nervous twitching of the eye, which must at once
strike the negro, who is particularly observant of
bodily defects. In view of the fondness of the
Swahilis for word-painting, this explanation seems
quite intelligible. The first version is, of course,
more agreeable to him.

Soon after the conclusion of peace Tippoo Tib
began his march back to the coast. He took his
way through Urungu to Mambwe, and from there
turned aside to Ruemba to fetch his brother Muhammed, whom he had left there. The inhabitants
of the countries he passed through everywhere
met him amicably. The news that he had beaten

Nsama, who was reputed invincible, had spread with lightning rapidity in all the adjacent districts, and all exerted themselves to win the favour of the victor. Carriers placed themselves readily at his disposal to carry the captured treasures from place to place. After the return from Ruemba the march was at once continued to Unyamwanga, Ujika, and Usafa, until at last they arrived again at Urori.

Until then the inhabitants of the districts traversed had performed the duties of carriers, but now it proved impossible to obtain the requisite number of men for the further march to the coast. Tippoo Tib therefore proceeded to Tabora to enlist carriers. When he arrived there he found the town deserted by the Arabs. His father, whom he would have liked to see again after years of separation, had gone on business to Kabwirr; his remaining compatriots had gone to war. Relations between them and Sultan Mkasiva were again strained.

Tippoo Tib dismounted at his stepmother Karunde's, and was received by her with all honour. The only Arab remaining in Tabora, Suud bin Said el Maamri, brother of a rich merchant still living in Zanzibar, urged him to take up his abode with him, and only after a long competition between his two entertainers for Tippoo Tib's coveted person, did the latter decide in favour of the more interesting company of his compatriot. Two days later the Arabs returned from their expedition. They had been beaten and had lost their leader. They were consequently in a very depressed state of mind. Tippoo Tib quickly engaged the necessary carriers, and after waiting two months longer to no purpose for

his father to come back, returned to Urori. Here
a painful surprise awaited him. His confidential
agent from Mbwa Maji had almost entirely made
away with the merchandise entrusted to him to the
value of 6,000 dollars ; only two slave-girls were
forthcoming, who had evidently pleased him and,
as love is proverbially blind, had been bought by
him at the unusual rate of 20 *frasilas* of ivory. To
the experienced business eye of Tippoo Tib this
seemed unheard-of, and he angrily chained up the
amorous youth. After four days he set him free
again, philosophically remarking to himself : ' He
who beats himself must not cry.' For that matter,
things had gone no better with his brother Muhammed bin Masud. His trusted agent had also made
away with a considerable fortune, but managed to
escape responsibility by falling ill of the small-pox
and dying.

After the pang of this unexpected loss had been
got over the march to the coast began, the objective
this time being Dar-es-Salaam. According to the
custom still observed, the caravan spent the last
night in the immediate neighbourhood of the town,
so as to make its entry the next day quite fresh and
in good order. On the 22nd day of Ramadhan, the
sacred month of fasting of Islam, they had their
last bivouac. At Dar-es-Salaam they found great
changes.

Sultan Seyyid Majid, who with right judgment
had realized that the basis of his power lay on the
mainland which furnished him with his wealth, had
determined to transfer his seat of government to
Dar-es-Salaam, and already begun to build a palace

worthy of himself there. Even before it was finished he spent yearly several months on the mainland, and the great importance attached by him to his plan is shown by the fact that he was staying there even in the month when the Arab usually retires into meditative seclusion, for he promised himself a great future for his rule from the place. True, he was unable to carry out his plans. A few years later he died suddenly, and with him vanished the interest in the further building up of the sovereignty on the mainland. The palace, whose erection he had so energetically begun, remained incomplete, like many private houses in Zanzibar started with insufficient means, and at last fell into a heap of ruins, the remains of which can still be traced near the hospital. If Majid had lived and been able to carry out his ambitious plans on the mainland, those daring expeditions of Dr. Peters and his companions to the Hinterland districts, which have led to the acquisition of a German colony in East Africa, would scarcely have been undertaken.

But for the time being things were lively at Dares-Salaam. All who belonged to 'society' had proceeded with the Sultan's Court to the new capital. All the non-trading Consuls and a great number of other Europeans, all the better-class Arabs from Zanzibar, Pemba, Mombasa, and Lamu, as well as a great body of Indians, had followed the Sovereign. Among the latter were all the creditors of Tippoo Tib, in whom the arrival of the caravan naturally evoked great delight; for on seeing the rich spoil in ivory they felt certain of receiving back the money they had advanced with high interest. But beside

this the coming of the caravan excited the greatest
interest in all circles as being the first one bound for
the coast to reach the new capital.   The Sultan himself showed interest in the daring voyager, whom he
loaded with high honours and entertained as his
guest until the ' Great Feast,' which concludes the
month of fasting (known in Turkey as the ' Festival
of Bairam ').

After the feast the whole Court returned to Zanzibar in three ships, headed by the Sultan and his
notables and the foreign representatives on board a
French man-of-war, while the remaining Arabs and
the Indians followed in two smaller vessels.

CHAPTER IV

' Per angusta ad augusta.'

AT Zanzibar there set in for Tippoo Tib, after his
long years of wandering, a period of refreshment,
which he could make as pleasant as he pleased now
that he had grown rich in money and honours. But
just as the European upon whom has once shone
the tropical sun of Africa, like the moth that flies to
the candle, ever feels drawn again to the land of
palms, so the traveller who had grown used to life
in the wilderness could not long endure the leisured
repose of the city. After a few months he is again
revolving fresh plans of travel, which are supported
by the Sultan himself, who naturally would only be
too glad if the distant interior were opened up as far
as possible by Arabs. In the first place, it brought
to the country rich produce in ivory and slaves, and
then it increased the political influence of the Sultan
that as many as possible of his subjects should
achieve importance in the interior. He therefore
offered Tippoo Tib financial support as well, by
directing the banyans who depended on him to give
him credit up to any desired extent.

'Banyan' is a generic name, under which in
East Africa are classed all heathen Indians. They
are divided into a great number of castes, of which
the highest is that of the priests, or Brahmins.
The other higher castes, of which especially the
Batias and Wanyans are represented here, are all
traders, and for the most part enjoy great prosperity, which it must be admitted they have not
always earned in an irreproachable way. They are
in part great usurers, and enrich themselves in that
capacity by advances on land at high interest.
But there are also very respectable banyans, who
have earned their wealth in an honourable manner.
For instance, the then head of the Batia community, Porsitom Tokarsi,* was highly respected
among Europeans and natives. The Ivory King,
Ratu Bimji, at Zanzibar, is also reputed a trustworthy man of business.

Seyyid Majid had farmed the Customs to the then
head of these banyans, one Ladda Damji. This
man had grown most independent in his office and
acted quite arbitrarily, as the Sultan did not trouble
himself about internal affairs so long as he received
his rent regularly. The farmer was, like his predecessor in the Gospel, a sinner. Among the Arabs
whom he had managed to make dependent on him
he was little loved. This Ladda, then—for so the
Sultan desired—was to advance Tippoo Tib the
money for a new journey. The latter did not like
this at all; he would much rather have borrowed
of his former business friends, the Muhammedan
Indians, but he did not dare to go counter to the

* Since dead.

will of the ruler, and so he agreed, submitting for
the time with Oriental equanimity. After a time
the Lord might yet order everything according to his
desires.

So a year went by, till Tippoo Tib was weary
of inaction, and forged serious plans of travel.
Heedless of his promise to Seyyid Majid, he turned
to those who had previously given him credit, Nur
Muhammed and Warsi Adwani, and declared to
them he wanted to travel again, but was tired
of borrowing, as before, of Tom and Harry. If they
wanted to remain in commercial association with
him, they must alone advance him the necessary
goods. They replied that they could not supply all he
wanted themselves, but that they would obtain what
was wanted from Taria Topan (then an all-powerful
Indian merchant, who later received an English
title, and was called Sir Taria). On no account was
he to have dealings with the banyan. But they
delayed from day to day, while Ladda kept
approaching Tippoo Tib with fresh offers of credit.
At last Tippoo Tib entered into negotiations with
him, and at once was assured of a credit of 50,000
dollars. Tippoo Tib proudly remarks on this : 'And
I had at that time not a plantation nor a house in
Zanzibar or anywhere else in the world ; but,' he
adds, ' I had a wife in Zanzibar, Bint Satum bin
Abdallah el Barwanie, who had much property in
Zanzibar and Muscat.' The latter circumstance
certainly did not weigh with the banyan, for
he knew well enough that, in case things went
wrong with Tippoo Tib, she would not have come
forward with a *pesa* to cover his losses. He must

have reckoned on Kismet and Tippoo Tib's star, and have also secretly cherished the hope that if he lost all his money, the Sultan, who had caused him to give the credit, would not leave him in the lurch.

So Tippoo Tib went to the hated banyan, and received on the first day 6,000 dollars' worth of goods. When the carriers were going with them to his house, Warsi Adwani spied them out, and with all the jealousy of a rival at once asked for whom the things were. On their replying that they belonged to Tippoo Tib, he rushed straight to Taria Topan to carry him the melancholy news. Taria was no less incensed, and called Tippoo Tib to account, asking him how he could go to the banyans when he (Taria) had placed his whole credit at his disposal and commissioned Warsi Adwani to tell him so; he must just take the goods back to the banyan as speedily as possible.

This proposal, however, was more easily made than carried out. Ladda, of course, would not hear of taking the things back again. At last Tippoo Tib had recourse to the plan of putting forward his relative Juma bin Sef bin Juma, who was to take the goods already delivered and some more as well. Tippoo Tib, to be sure, had to be security for him with Ladda. Hereupon Taria also hastened to deliver his supplies. It was the first time that he had lent on so insecure an enterprise as a caravan journey into the interior—a proof of how much confidence people placed in Tippoo Tib's spirit of adventure.

Soon 200 loads were corded, which were sent

4

on before to Ituru, the place of residence of old
Muhammed. Tippoo Tib himself still remained in
the city, in order to procure the substance which
would ensure the success of his journey—the indis-
pensable gunpowder. This was before the Brussels
agreement, and gunpowder was to be got easily
and cheaply, 26 lbs. costing 4 dollars. He bought
in round numbers 5,000 dollars' worth, or over 300
hundredweight! He unconcernedly stored it in his
house, which stood in the midst of the European
quarter, and left it there for ten days, until he
could ship it in dhows to Bagamoyo. But this
light-hearted carelessness was not to be without
its sequel.

A month had passed since the shipment, when
suddenly one evening two Arabs appeared at his
house to summon him next morning before Sleman
bin Ali, the Sultan's minister. With the cheerful-
ness of an easy conscience, our hero set off to see the
dignitary, who asked him with an official air if it
was he who had stored powder in the neighbourhood of the English Consulate. He calmly answered
'Yes'; which made the minister ask the further
question whether Tippoo Tib had gone mad. 'No,'
replied he; 'I am in full possession of my senses.'
After this somewhat vague introduction the minister
proceeded to deliver a long harangue as to its being
quite illegal to bring powder into the city, and so
endanger the lives and limbs of the inhabitants.
Tippoo Tib assured him he had had no idea of it;
he had been years in the interior, and as a free man
of course did not know the recent police regulations, but it should not happen again. But the

minister was not content with this bill drawn on
the future : ignorance of the law did not exempt
from punishment ; the offence had been committed
and called for retribution, the more so that the
English Consul had heard of the matter, and was
very indignant about it ; he was to come again
next morning and hear the sentence that Seyyid
Majid might pass on him.

When Tippoo Tib appeared accordingly, he was
informed that Seyyid Majid had not known that he
was the transgressor, but that the matter had been
mooted by the English Consul-General, and now he
must either be locked up for a month or pay the
price of the powder bought as a fine. Tippoo Tib
declared in favour of the latter. He estimated the
value somewhat vaguely as more than 4,000 dollars,
but he would rather pay the money than be confined
even for a few days. Touched by such self-sacrifice,
the minister advised him to allow himself to be
locked up quietly for two or three days, and afterwards the matter would settle itself.

So Tippoo Tib went to the prison, a solid four-
square building behind the toll-house, with a dirty
courtyard in the middle and a tower at each of the
corners, wrongly described as a Portuguese fort,
though in reality it was only built at the beginning
of last century by Seyyid Said. However, it was a
cheerful prison for Tippoo Tib. He was given a
decent room, in which he could do as he pleased.
During the day he received visitors, and at night his
wives kept him company.

The conditions have even now not changed
materially in this respect. A criminal who knows

how to get on well with his custodians can still
live pleasantly in Zanzibar Prison, if he does not
prefer to open the door of his dungeon with a golden
key.

When Tippoo Tib was set free on the third day,
he went to the English Consul-General, Sir John
Kirk, who asked him where he had been hidden so
long. He rejoined in dudgeon that he had been
locked up on account of the powder. This was
quite new to the Consul, who had indeed been angry
about the business, but had no idea that Tippoo Tib
was the culprit. Otherwise—so Tippoo Tib hints
—he would have winked at the incident, for he
valued him very much, since he had so chivalrously
espoused the cause of the Consul's friend Livingstone, and had brought important letters from him
to the Consulate.

Some weeks later Tippoo Tib proceeded to Bagamoyo to despatch further loads to the interior.
Even so goods to the amount of some 300 loads remained behind, which he requested Muhammed bin
Masud to make ready for conveyance. He himself
wanted first to go once more to Dar-es-Salaam, to
take leave of Seyyid Majid, who had returned there.
As he also had to take leave of his business friends
in Zanzibar, he instructed Muhammed to march on
in the meantime, and expect him in a few days at
Kwere, a place not far from Bagamoyo. His stay
in Zanzibar, however, lasted longer than he anticipated, for he had to be present at a marriage there at
the house of Rashid Adwani : both Oriental polite-
ness and business considerations prevented his
declining the invitation. Thus he was detained

against his will seventeen days longer than he
intended.

The consequence was that he found not a soul at
Kwere. Muhammed had got tired of waiting,
though he caught him up a few days later at
Usagara, and from there they continued their
journey together. But they had not got far up
country towards Ugogo when a great disaster
befell the caravan. Cholera broke out, and every
day several carriers died. Moreover, the country
presented many difficulties, for Ugogo was a poor
district, in which provisions were scarcely to be had,
especially as the population displayed hostility and
nowhere offered anything for sale. ' Wherever we
went,' complains Tippoo Tib, ' we were driven back.'
They had, it is true, to some extent supplied themselves at Usagara, but the provision taken with them
was long since exhausted.

While in this unenviable plight they encountered
on the highway one day, at the western limit of
Ugogo, a body of armed warriors, who sought to
bar their further progress. As disease was prevalent on the coast, the Shensis did not want
to let the travellers pass through their townships,
but urged them to march through the forest, and
rejoin the caravan road again only at Mgunda
Mkali, a steppe devoid of food or water and seven
days' march in extent. The plan would have meant
certain destruction, without provisions as they were
and with the epidemic raging in the caravan. So
a council of war was called. Tippoo Tib requested
his brother Muhammed, as the elder, to make the
decision. But Muhammed bowed to Tippoo Tib's

greater insight, and left to him the decision, which was in favour of forcing a passage. When this was communicated to the soldiers they begged for a short respite, so that they might report to their Sultan Kiuje. Soon they came back, and announced that free transit was granted them, but they must encamp outside the first town on the river, and strike camp again after two days. Provisions would be brought into their camp. The river by which they took ground, however, was no river, at least for the time, for all the water was dried up; but by digging vigorously some springs were discovered, from which a scanty supply of water was obtained. Meanwhile the disease continued its ravages.

When the caravan, after the two days' rest, reached the western frontier of Ugogo by a longish march, it was already so thinned that there were not enough carriers left. A great number of loads were therefore buried—of course, only such goods as a lengthy stay in the ground would not hurt : beads, lead for the guns, chains, and so on. They then made their way through the desolate wilderness, by the Mgunda Mkali to Tura, where various Arab caravans were encountered which had started at the same time from Bagamoyo, but had taken another route.

These also had had dismal experiences. They had dwindled by a third through disease, and had in consequence of the loss of carriers also lost much merchandise. An acquaintance from Tabora also turned up here—the Arab Nasor bin Masud—who had travelled to meet the much-damaged caravan

of a business friend, in order to save as much of it
as possible, as it had lost its leader through the
epidemic.

At Rubuga, a further stage, Tippoo Tib found
his old father, who had marched to meet him, and
awaited him here with the caravan that had gone
on before. It was the first meeting between father
and son after long years. Since the war with
Mnywa Sere, at the close of which Tippoo Tib had
journeyed to Urua, they had not seen each other.
' At that time I was still a poor and unknown man,
but many years have gone by since then,' says
Tippoo Tib in his biography, in proud recollection.
Together they entered Tabora, where our hero
naturally found many alterations.

A short time before his stepmother Karunde
had died, which caused the sorrowing widower,
Muhammed bin Juma, at once to look about him
for a new life-companion. There were enough
aspirants forthcoming for the hand of the powerful
chieftain, but he took into consideration only a
daughter of Mkasiva, and Nyaso, a younger daughter
of Fundi Kira. Mkasiva, who was very anxious to
bind old Muhammed to him by the closest bands of
relationship, left nothing untried to capture him as
a son-in-law. But at last Nyaso gained the victory;
and, writes Tippoo Tib, just as had been the case
with Karunde, so now again all the property, dead
or alive, in Tabora was Muhammed's. But he had
thus made an enemy of the ruler of the country—
Mkasiva—as was soon to be seen.

An elephant was killed by Muhammed's men
in the immediate neighbourhood of the town, whose

tusks attained the splendid weight of $5\frac{1}{4}$ *frasilas*.
Mkasiva, supported by the Vali Said bin Salum el
Lemki, maintained that the ivory was his, as the
elephant had been killed in his jurisdiction, and
demanded its surrender. Muhammed and his wife
Nyaso refused flatly, and now, after lengthy dis-
cussions, they were preparing to decide the point
at issue by a regular war, when a more serious
event suddenly reconciled the contending parties.

The Wangoni, a dreaded Wahehe tribe, threatened
to invade the country. They had been called in by
Mshama, a nephew of Mkasiva, who had himself
aimed at the throne, and being, therefore, perse-
cuted by his uncle, had fled to Uhehe, whence he
was now returning, breathing vengeance. The
enemy's hordes had already appeared in Njombo, a
district some three hours south of Tabora. A
force, hastily mustered from the people at Kwihara,
was sent against them without delay, under the
leadership of the Arab Abdallah bin Nasib, and
the more distant Arabs, amongst them Tippoo Tib,
received a summons to assemble at once at Kwihara.
From here they marched together after the advance
guard, which they found in Njombo almost totally
destroyed. They had been beaten by the Wangoni,
and of the Swahilis alone had lost fifty, besides
more than 100 Uganda men, who had happened to
be at Kwihara and took part in the expedition.
They had been sent by Sultan Mtesa to bring
presents to Seyyid Majid, in return for the ample
presents he had himself sent from Zanzibar.

After their victory over the Arab troops, the
Wangoni, who probably cared less about the pre-

tensions of Mshama to the throne than about
making a profitable raid, had retired with large
herds of cattle.   Tippoo Tib's proposal to follow
on their heels found no response amid the general
depression.   All retreated hastily to Tabora.   Here
Tippoo Tib once more unfolded his plans, and at
length, on the second day, carried his point — in
favour of immediate pursuit.   The avenging force
actually got as far as Msanga, in the immediate
neighbourhood of Njombo, when the heroes again
changed their minds and wheeled about towards
their homes and Penates.   Only Tippoo Tib and
another Arab named Said bin Habib continued the
march.   They advanced by Msuto, the western
frontier place of Unyanyembe, as far as the river
Njombo, which prevented any further pursuit.
They saw that the Wangoni had already too long
a start, and did not wish to expose themselves to
the danger of encountering the enemy in a strange
country, which, moreover, was divided from their
home by a body of water that was difficult to pass.
So they, too, returned to Tabora without having
accomplished anything.

Tippoo Tib wished not to stay there any longer,
but to go at once to Itahua, only the remaining
Arabs would not let him.   He must first wait and
see that the Wangoni did not return to the attack.
Now that they had gained an easy victory they
would no doubt take a fancy to the business, and
soon appear on a fresh raid.   ' The folks were simply
at that time not yet accustomed to war.'

Unwillingly Tippoo Tib gave way.   When two
months of waiting had passed quietly away, he sent

forward the greater part of his caravan to Itahua, and after another month a further instalment—all but a small portion, which remained behind under his own orders. Meanwhile, he had sent to Ugogo to have the buried goods fetched. They were fortunately found almost complete, except that a small portion of the beads had been lost in the sand. When they arrived, Tippoo Tib got under way, in spite of the persuasions of his fellow-tribesmen, who would have liked to keep him with them for their own safety, and made his first halt in Ugalla, a district lying to the south-west.

CHAPTER V

' El ein bil ein wa 'l anf bil anf wa 'l udhn bil udhn wa 's sin bis sin.'

An eye for an eye, a nose for a nose, an ear for an ear, a tooth for a tooth.

KORAN : *Suret el Maide*, v. 45.

UGALLA was nominally ruled by a certain Taka as Sultan, in reality, however, by his younger brother Rijowe, who, according to Tippoo Tib's descriptions, was a great tyrant and created all possible difficulties for travellers. He lived in a large town which was strongly fortified with ramparts and ditches. He allowed the caravan to pitch its camp outside the fortress at a distance of a quarter of an hour. Tippoo Tib wanted to buy in his country sufficient provisions for eight days, which he required for his march to Ukonongo, but he did not obtain permission to do so until he had paid five oxen and a hundred garments. Thereupon he was allowed to make his purchases and handed over to his men their provisions in the shape of *mtama* (native corn), which they at once began to pound, partly in the camp, partly in the town itself. Unfortunately this corn was destined to be an apple of discord.

On the morning of the second day Tippoo Tib was summoned to an audience with the Sultan. With a following of sixteen men, who as a precaution had with them guns loaded with ball, he betook himself to the town. On the way he met one of his Swahilis, who told him furiously that a savage had spilled all his corn and belaboured him with his fists ; he was going now to fetch his gun and meant to avenge himself on the ruffian. Tippoo Tib tried to induce him by persuasion to refrain from such disorderly methods, which would place them all in a most awkward position ; it was a matter of importance to him to preserve peace, and he would gladly replace the spilled corn. Apparently satisfied, the young man withdrew, while Tippoo Tib proceeded with his attendants to the Sultan's house. The latter greeted the strangers and conducted them to the dwelling of his principal wife, where they were to wait outside a few minutes. Meantime the injured Swahili came by, just as he had at first said, armed with his musket. Tippoo Tib called him to him and dealt him several fatherly boxes on the ear— six or seven, so far as he remembers. But the chastisement came too late. The Shensis had already seen him and realized from the situation that he meant to be revenged on them. They raised a furious shout and charged in on Tippoo Tib and his men. In the rain of spears and arrows a slave of Tippoo Tib's fell.

Tippoo Tib turned to the Sultan and called on him to control his subjects. But whether he felt himself powerless in face of the excited mob or was himself a party to the breach of the peace, he simply took to flight, but did not get far, being immediately brought down by a shot from the Arabs, who were now on their part using their weapons. At sight of their falling chieftain the savages took to flight.

But the Arabs, who remained on the spot, did not feel comfortable. The town was everywhere strongly fortified, and the concealed enemy might be lying in wait anywhere. They made in a body for the nearest gate—of which there were six—and returned to their camp outside the town. They found it quite deserted. Even the two sentries had disappeared. But as they stood between fear and hope at the main gate, which lay opposite their camp, a troop of people came suddenly towards them from within, headed by the red flag.* They had searched the town through and scarcely found a living soul. They brought with them only six women as prisoners of war.

Then Tippoo Tib went back into the town to reconnoitre. It was quite deserted by the men, but sixty more women were found and welcomed as good booty. Also what merchandise and ivory they found—it was not much—was thankfully accepted. After Tippoo Tib had become master of the field of battle he determined to camp inside the town, in order to secure himself against a more than probable attempt at revenge. He therefore summoned his people living outside in the villages by sound of drum, and in doing so again had the pleasant surprise of finding that a great portion of his brave

* In Africa every large caravan still bears the flag of its nationality. That of Zanzibar is blood red.

fellows had vanished. No less than sixty Wanyamwezi were not forthcoming. If they had been killed
their bodies would have been found ; so it was
quite clear that they had shown the white feather
at the beginning of the fight. It was not far to their
home at Tabora (five days' easy march without
loads).

Under these circumstances it was not possible at
once to continue the journey. Yet even if they
determined to remain it was not easy to know what
to do. Should they start in pursuit of the Shensis
or remain idly sitting till they returned with reinforcements to attack them ? Against the former
the prudent Said bin Ali gave his voice ; if the
fighting men went out in pursuit the loads would
still have to be left behind. Then how easily, when
the Arabs had marched out, could the Shensis
double back on the town another way and cut down
the camp followers there !

So they stayed, and had not to wait long before
the natives came back. On the eighth day, shortly
before sunrise, when the Arabs were just at their
first prayer, they heard the clamour of the advancing
hordes. These were driven back with a few well-
aimed volleys, and pursued for two hours. On the
side of the Shensis some seventy men had fallen ;
the Arabs had only four killed and six wounded.

After eight days more they again heard the noise
of an advancing host. The fear that it was a
renewal of the attack was, however, not well-
grounded. They were men from Tabora, who had
been sent by the Vali, at Seyyid Majid's instance, to
Uganda. They brought with them letters from the

Vali and old Muhammed containing favourable news. They had heard through the fugitive Wan-yamwezi, who had in fact fled back to Tabora, of the conflicts at Ugalla. Later on Sultan Rijowe had sought refuge with them, in order to obtain peace with Tippoo Tib by their intercession. Now the Vali and Muhammed wanted to come themselves to set matters in the right channel. Four days later they came, and were received outside the town by Tippoo Tib. But they would not make their entry until he had declared his readiness for the conclusion of peace. Tippoo Tib agreed and accepted beforehand the conditions they might regard as right. After their entry they came to an agreement that Tippoo Tib should give back the women he had taken, while the Shensis were only to pay compensation for those who had fallen on the side of the Arabs.

So peace was concluded. As the fugitive Wanyamwezi had come back with the Arabs from Tabora, there was nothing more to hinder the march. They moved by Ukonongo to Fipa, Sultan Karagwe's country. Here they rejoined their friends, who had gone on in advance, with Muhammed bin Masud at their head. These had found the country, which enjoyed great fertility, so pleasant that they had determined to await the rearguard there. They had only sent on one of their number, Juma bin Sef bin Juma, to Itahua. Tippoo Tib remained in Fipa six days, to provision his caravan in this fertile region for the impending march through more barren tracts; then they set off together—a column 4,000 strong. The way led along the shores of Lake Tanganyika, and presented many difficulties. The country there is very mountainous, and so they went up hill and down dale till at last they reached Urungu—an impoverished district, which they soon left again, as provisions were not to be had.

At last they reached the district of Itahua, and came to a town where Mkura, a son of Nsama, ruled. Here there was again great plenty, especially an astonishing crop of manioc, with which the famished carriers greedily repaid themselves for the privations of the past weeks. Some days later the whole band sickened with violent dysentery, to which forty men fell victims. Fortunately the Arab Juma bin Sef, who was trading in Itahua, appeared soon after with a remedy for the disease. He had a pungent curry sauce, stirred up with pepper and muscat, which he gave the men to eat with lean goat's flesh. This was given the patients for several days, and the homely remedy really had its effect. The dysentery gradually ceased, though the men were much exhausted for a long time after. The disease was not, however, as Juma taught them, caused solely by their voracity, but the manioc was of a different kind from what they had hitherto been accustomed. It was extraordinarily bitter, and only innocuous when it had been steeped for a considerable time in water, then allowed to dry for several days, and finally cooked. This Tippoo Tib's men, of course, did not know, and even if they had known it they would probably not have observed the precaution, for in the eight days which they would have needed to make the manioc

fit for use they would very likely have starved.
They had not even taken the trouble to cook it,
but consumed it raw, just as it came out of the
ground.

When the caravan had recovered, they proceeded
further to seek out their old acquaintance Nsama.
To all the Arabs he gave a friendly reception, only he
refused to see Tippoo Tib. He sent, however, forty
elephant's tusks, of a weight of 65 *frasilas*, as a
present to his guest, but added that that was all
the ivory he had. The assurance sounded scarcely
credible, for shortly before he had sold to Juma bin
Sef 300 *frasilas*, besides which the country swarmed
with elephants. Tippoo Tib's men employed themselves busily in hunting. In particular, there were
three of his slaves who distinguished themselves in
woodcraft. He had bought them long before, almost
against his will, from a bankrupt named Shihiri,
who wanted money and offered him four men, the
lot for 100 dollars (about 300 marks). One of them
had escaped in Ugogo ; the remainder now brought
in their purchase-money, with interest. It was no
rare occurrence for them to secure twenty tusks
in one morning. There were also buffaloes in
abundance, which were hunted for the sake of their
meat.

As Tippoo Tib could not hope for much from
a further stay near his old enemy, he left his
hunters behind and went on to Ruemba, where
Sultans Mwamba, Kitimkaro, and Shanza ruled.
For but a small amount of goods he obtained a
great deal of ivory, wherefore he bears witness
that they were good people. He returned once

5

more with his treasures to Itahua, where he now
concocted a fresh plan. Muhammed bin Masud
was to remain with the bulk of the merchandise in
the country, while Tippoo Tib purposed, taking all
the beads that the two had with them, to proceed
westwards to Urua, where beads were fetching high
prices.

Their way led them through the once powerful
and still very important Kasembe kingdom of
Lunda, which at the end of the eighteenth century
had been visited by Portuguese discoverers, and
in 1866 and 1867 was systematically explored by
Livingstone. It is a fertile plateau to the west of
Lake Mueru, bounded on the north by Itahua and
Kabwire, on the south and east by Lombemba and
Kisinga. The country was governed by elected
rulers called Kasembe, a word that, according to
Livingstone, signifies 'general.' The Kasembes
seem to have changed very often, as they were
deposed as soon as they became unpopular. The
ruler whom Livingstone found there in 1867 was
called Maonga, and was the seventh Kasembe; but
his predecessor, Lekwisa, was still alive, and in
exile with Nsama. Livingstone visited Maonga on
November 28, 1867, in his capital at the north end
of Mofwe—a lake abounding in fish, formed by the
Luapula above the larger and better known Mueru.
Each Kasembe used to found a separate town as his
place of residence. The capital of the then reigning
Kasembe covered an area of an English square mile,
on which some hundreds of huts lay scattered
among cassava plantations. The court of the ruler
—many would have called it a palace—formed a

quadrangle 300 ells in length and 200 in breadth,
and was surrounded by a high bamboo hedge.
Men's skulls were displayed here and there as a
decoration. A great portion of the people had
cropped ears and lopped-off arms—mutilations which
were not inflicted on the subjects for æsthetic
reasons, as in the case of fox-terriers with us, but
only to furnish them with a life-long reminder that
their ruler had once been obliged to give expression
to his disapproval of their conduct.

The first impression was not by any means re-
assuring to the visitor, but he was soon compensated
for the feeling of horror which came over him on
entering by the amusing spectacle which presented
itself as he went further. Before his hut, on a
couch of lion and leopard skins, sat a figure with a
squinting face, wrapped in a coarse garment of
white and blue striped material, with a red border
bunched out voluminously, so that he looked as if he
had put on a crinoline the wrong way about. The
arms, feet, and head were clad in sleeves, trousers,
and cap, with a beautiful pattern of coloured beads,
while this strange fashion-block was crowned with
an aigrette of yellow feathers. The grandees of
the kingdom, shaded by huge patched umbrellas,
approached their master respectfully, bowing cere-
moniously before him, and then took their places
on his right. Livingstone was presented by a
minister with cropped ears to the Kasembe, who,
after being briefly informed as well as might be of
the purpose and aim of the explorer's journey, was
pleased to accept his presents. As they partly
consisted of grotesque garments, he was highly

delighted, which did not hinder him from requiting them with nothing but a lean goat and a few fish. At a subsequent audience he was openly mocked for his meanness by the Arab Muhammed bin Saleh, who had lived ten years in the country.

Livingstone has no high opinion of the power of the Kasembe of his day. He thinks if he had to summon the array for war, he would scarcely be able to get together 1,000 vagabonds, whereas the first Portuguese visitor, Pereira, records that the Kasembe he found there had a standing army of 20,000 trained warriors. Livingstone has the impression that he could have established friendly relations with Maonga, whom he lectured on the iniquity of the slave trade, only the sight of his squinting eyes and the many mutilated people always deterred him.

When Tippoo Tib came into the country some years had passed since then, and another Kasembe was already on the throne. The entry into Lunda did not take the form of a welcome to him. Amid heavy rainstorms, which allowed the great caravan to progress but slowly, they reached the frontier of Itahua. On the way they had received the consoling intelligence that Nsama, after Tippoo Tib's departure, had exhibited great stores of ivory, which he had been unwilling to show his conqueror, but which the Arabs now could purchase at their ease. The boundary between Itahua and Lunda was formed by a river, which, owing to the rainy season, was greatly swollen. The caravan had to march a great distance upstream before it could ford it. As the leading files reached the land they were

attacked by the Walunda, who struck down four
men and took a quantity of merchandise and
muskets. As the Kasembe was at enmity with
Nsama and had no reason for treating Tippoo Tib,
who was well enough known as an opponent of
Nsama's, in an unfriendly way, this reception was
most startling, and our traveller resolved, before
retaliating, to inquire into the causes of this unexpected hostility. He was haughtily answered
that the Walunda had attacked the Arabs' followers
quite deliberately, for they had boasted that they
had defeated Nsama, and now they, Kasembe's men,
would show them they were something different,
and had determined to strike down every intruder
into their country. This impudent reply demanded
immediate retribution. Even Said bin Ali el
Hinawi was of this opinion—a *mutawa*,* a pious and
forgiving man who had once stood in high honour
in Zanzibar, but later, as an adherent of Burghash,
fell into disfavour with Seyyid Majid, and when the
latter so far humiliated him as to give him a box on
the ears, retired in dudgeon and went on his travels.
In spite of all, he had retained his pious disposition,
and was always ready to give good advice when it
was possible ; but now even he advised fighting.
More troops were sent for in haste from Itahua ; the
river forming the frontier was crossed, and in a few

---

* Literally, ' a very obedient.' The people are so called
who devote themselves to a specially religious way of life.
They wear as a badge the white turban, which many certainly
assume without being entitled to do so ; *e.g.*, the well-known
Wali Sleman bin Nasor always wears it, though, in view of
his unprejudiced attitude towards the prohibition of wine-
drinking, he has no claim to the distinction.

months all Lunda was subjugated. The Kasembe
—Tippoo Tib did not remember his name—was
driven from the country, and a new chief named
Mabote set up in his place. This man had been
Kasembe once before, but had been deposed by his
people because he refused to submit to circumcision,
which was not otherwise customary in the country,
but was expected of its rulers.

CHAPTER VI

ENTRY INTO URUA

'Duobus certantibus gaudet tertius.'

AFTER thus subduing the mighty kingdom of
Lunda, they proceeded next in a northerly direction along Lake Mueru, until they reached the
capital of Sultan Mpueto. Here the Congo issues
from the lake under the name of Luapula. The
river there is of course narrow, and was easily
crossed in boats. On the left bank lay Urua, the
objective of the travellers. At first not much was
to be discovered of the much-boasted power of the
country. The natives were weak in bodily structure,
frequently disfigured by goitres, and immoderately
addicted to the enjoyment of tobacco and hemp, a
passion which procured them from their western
neighbours, to whom smoking seemed contemptible,
the nickname Wahemba : *watumwa vuaka*—*i.e.*,
slaves of tobacco. As their country adjoined
those of the marauding Nsama and Kasembe, they
were, of course, exposed to constant unexpected
attacks, and were thus rendered specially timid and
suspicious. Moreover, the natural conformation of
their territory tended to impose the defensive on
them. The country was rich in caves, which ran far

71

into the mountains and offered ample shelter to several hundred men. As they were stalactite formations, there was no want of water inside them. Provisions could be taken into them to any amount desired, and, when the times were warlike, were stored up there beforehand. Tippoo Tib recounts his visit to such a cave, which had two entrances and at the largest point was some 12 feet wide. He went in with candles, but contented himself with examining the cavern. His uncle, Bushir bin Habib, had more pluck, and came out at the other end of the mountain, after a long progress through dark passages.

In case of war these caves, of course, afforded an excellent refuge. On the enemy's approach all the townships were deserted, and the inhabitants vanished from the soil. Later on Msire, Sultan of Katanga, which lay to the south-west, fathomed the secret, and, as later conquerors have dealt with similar troglodytes, smoked them out like a fox from his earth. He placed burning wood before one opening and let the smoke penetrate, until the cave-dwellers came out on the other side and submitted.

On pursuing his march, Tippoo Tib came upon a Sultan named Kajumbe. His subjects were stronger men than the Warua of the frontier, and he himself, who, on account of his imperiousness, bore the surname Kha Ukuma, the Swashbuckler, wielded considerable power, which he made the newcomers feel. For all the ivory which they pur-chased they had to pay a high duty, which was here called *kiremba*. At the same time, the yield of ivory of the country was slight and the natives hard to deal with. A bargain over a single tusk often lasted for several days.

Thus the news came most opportunely that in rather more distant regions far more favourable conditions of trade prevailed. Two Sultans, named Mrongo Tambwe and Mrongo Kassanga, sent messengers to Tippoo Tib, who brought him several tusks as a present and said that in their country there was plenty of ivory; if that was what Tippoo Tib wanted he had only to come to them. But they dared not bring it for exchange into Kajumbe's territory, for, warned by previous experiences, they feared that most of it would be stolen from them.

Even Msire, the great Sultan of Katanga, sent an embassy of homage with twelve elephant's tusks. He had heard that Tippoo Tib had passed triumphantly through Nsama's and Kasembe's country, and was now afraid lest the mighty conqueror should make war against him too. Our traveller, who to be sure had as yet entertained no such thought, at once took advantage of this favourable frame of mind and sent an answer that such was certainly his intention. 'It is true, I have heard that he is a very bad man and attacks people without cause. If necessary, I will come and chastise him—unless he sends twenty more tusks beside these.'

Much alarmed by these haughty words, Msire's people departed, taking with them, if possible, a still higher opinion of the intruder than they had before.

To get away, to be sure, was not such a simple matter. Kasembe, in fact, cherished the opinion that travellers who came into his country were bound

to dispose of all their goods there. How long they
took about it did not matter to him if they only paid
plenty of duty. Tippoo Tib, however, did not feel
disposed, with his rich supplies of beads, to wait
there whole decades for ivory that might or might
not come, and as peaceful negotiations were of no
avail, he made his exit by force. After an hour's
fighting the Warua took to flight, and the next
morning Kajumbe sued for peace, which was granted
him in return for nine elephant's tusks.

Three days later they came upon a Sultan named
Mseka, in whose village a two days' halt was made.
During this sojourn envoys came once more from
Mrongo Tambwe, who sent presents of ivory and
again invited the travellers to visit his country.
Tippoo Tib replied it did not matter to him where
he went if there was only ivory, and followed his
emissaries.

After two days' march the guides halted at some
cross-roads and announced that from there there
were two ways: the one led through uninhabited,
waterless jungle, but had the advantage of security;
if they took the more convenient path through inhabited places, they would have to be constantly
fighting. The position was as follows : the country
for which they were making stretched along Lake
Kissale, a broad, swamp-like continuation of the
Lualaba. This lake was the very life of the country.
It was abundantly rich in fish, and yielded its
inhabitants, without difficulty, ample sustenance.
There were also endless swarms of wild ducks,
which it was not difficult to bring down. Nay, this
beneficent lake was made subservient even to

elephant-hunting. The forests were beaten and the mighty pachyderms driven towards the water. There they lost themselves in the muddy, reed-grown banks, and the natives, hastening to the spot in boats, killed them with spears without difficulty.

No wonder, then, that rich settlements with a brisk traffic sprang up round this lake. People came from far and wide to barter for its products. In exchange for the fish, which, when dried, were exported long distances, they brought the produce of their own districts. The chief articles of barter were the so-called *viramba*, stuffs woven out of the bark of trees, such as are still often seen in East Africa, imported from Madagascar. These stuffs were then worn throughout Manyemaland, and had such a universally acknowledged value that they were regarded as a substitute for money. Another important article was a kind of tree-oil.

In this favoured country, once peacefully united under one sceptre, two near relatives had for many years been striving for the mastery, Mrongo Tambwe and Mrongo Kassanga. First one was victorious, then the other. The victor always took up his residence on the lake, while the conquered fled into the jungle until he was once more strong enough to attack and overcome his rival. The part of the conquered was being played just at that time by Tambwe, which was why he had been in such a hurry to secure the friendship of the newcomer.

To Tippoo Tib it was of course a most welcome state of things that he could intervene in the internal affairs of the country with a certain show of right, and it was especially to his advantage that, since the two rivals were about equally strong, he must, by interposing with his seasoned troops, splendidly armed as compared with the savages, infallibly decide the matter. He therefore had not the slightest intention of acting on the proposal of the Warua guides, and stealing by the forest route to Tambwe. But as the Warua did not dare to follow him on the way through the towns, he took only two of them with him as guides, but dressed them up, for the sake of their peace of mind, in Swahili clothes, so that they might not be recognised by their enemies.

They at once entered fertile, richly populated districts, in which one township succeeded another. They pitched their camp in a town five hours' march from the lake. Mrongo Kassanga, who was himself sojourning on the lake, sent envoys to them, asking them to pay him a visit the next day. The answer was they were on the way to Mrongo Tambwe, and had nothing to do with him. ' Yes,' answered Kassanga's men, ' he was somewhere in the wilderness, and had been driven out by them. If they insisted on going to their enemy, they would be attacked and overcome.' Nor were hostilities long in ensuing. In the afternoon some members of the caravan were attacked while fetching water, and their utensils stolen. Tippoo Tib, who was eager to attack at once, allowed himself to be per-suaded by the milder Said bin Ali to keep the peace for the time. He determined to demand an explana-tion from Mrongo Kassanga next morning.

In the night, however, it was clear that the natives were planning war. All round drums sounded, which, as the Warua they had with them recognised from the sound, were summoning the people to battle. When the caravan was getting under way next morning it was attacked. The onslaught, however, was successfully repulsed. Some townships were set on fire, and several hundred prisoners taken.

Next morning, quite early, the drums again sounded. The Arabs were afraid that this meant a fresh attack, but their guides assured them that these were the drums of Mrongo Tambwe's followers. Presently 500 men arrived, and brought the news that their master was just making his entry into the townships on the lake, and begged his Arab friends to meet him in the capital. When, after a fair fight, it was again Tambwe's turn, the natives were soon on the scene again, and commerce flourished as in the days of his exiled rival. The new Sultan showed himself very friendly towards his foreign allies. In particular he sent them daily boatloads of fish.

However pleasant life on the lake might be, it did not offer what the travellers sought first and foremost. There was much less ivory here than even in Kajumbe's territory. Then Tippoo Tib heard that there was probably a great deal in a country called Irande. The news was indeed not fully vouched for, for other informants reported, on the contrary, that there was no trade there in ivory—only in stuffs made of tree-bark. Tippoo Tib said to himself, however, that a country into which no freeborn man had penetrated since the Creation must certainly harbour ivory, and set off.

Shortly before their departure emissaries again
came from Msire to entice the travellers into his
country. To the inquiry what objects of barter
were most attractive there, they replied that European stuffs were in request. As Tippoo Tib had
only beads with him, Said bin Ali was told off for
the journey to Katanga. He had at the time been
unable to make up his mind, like the other Arabs,
to leave his stuffs behind in Nsama's country, and
now hoped to make his fortune out of the loads that
had been so long dragged with him for nothing.
As soon as his trading was concluded, he was to
return to the Arabs who had remained at Itahua.

So Said proceeded southwards, protected by
thirty muskets. Tippoo Tib advanced further into
the unknown west. Guided by some men of Mrongo
Tambwe's, he crossed the Lualaba, but soon turned
back when he heard that an acquaintance of his—
Juma bin Salum—was staying in the neighbourhood near the capital of a chief named Kirua. This
Arab, generally known by the sobriquet of Juma
Mericano,* and so styled in many books of travel
by European explorers, was one of the oldest
traders in the interior of Africa. As early as 1858
Burton and Speke, the daring discoverers of Lake
Tanganyika, had come across him at Ujiji. He had
since then carried on trade uninterruptedly in
Itahua, Lunda, and Katanga, and since the early
seventies had kept a standing camp near Kirua on
Lake Usenge. The traveller Cameron found him

---

* Mericano was originally a cotton material imported only
from America. Juma was so called because he dealt principally
in it.

in October, 1874—somewhat later than the occurrences here described—at his fortified settlement, Kilemba, in Kassanga's country, and describes him as a 'handsome, dignified man,' and the most amiable and hospitable of the Arab traders in Africa with whom he came in close contact.

Tippoo Tib endeavoured to get his friend to accompany him on his journey to Irande, but met with no response. Juma Mericano took the ground that a certain profit on a small scale was preferable to the uncertain expectation of great wealth, and crowned his objections by declaring that he could not enter a country in which no Arab had yet set foot. Tippoo Tib called him a coward and started off alone. The ivory he had so far acquired— 300 *frasilas*—he left behind.

On entering Irande there was at first not much sign of ivory, but, on the other hand, the country offered all the more interest in other respects. As to the impressions he received there and the occurrences that ensued, we will let him give his own account in the next chapter.

CHAPTER VII

' May one deceive the people ?
I say not so.
Yet if you must delude them,
Be it not too subtly done.'
GOETHE : *Epigrams.*

' THE towns of the country were astonishingly large
and their number boundless. Their business is
to weave *viramba.* They build their towns in such
a way that there is a row of houses here and another
row there, like the rows of clove-trees. In the
middle there remains a vacant space, which is
some 40 ells wide, or perhaps more, and the
number of the houses is fifty here and fifty there.
In the middle they build a remarkably big house
with a *barasa*, in which all the craftsmen assemble
to weave *viramba.* One may walk in a town for
six, seven, or eight hours. All their towns are
built in the same way : a row of houses here, and
another row there, and in the middle the work
barasa. So we marched about the land of Irande,
and however long we waited and inquired for trade
in ivory, there was nothing but *viramba.* And in
this country they knew nothing of freeborn men, nor

80

at that time did they know of guns. The Warua went into this country and brought fish there to purchase *viramba*, and if they saw ivory they at once obtained it at a low price ; only there was no ivory. And the Warua had no guns ; they had only bows and arrows as weapons ; guns they did not know. They asked if the guns we had were *mituwangu*, which means "rammers." We said "Yes," and they thought they were rammers. So we journeyed until we came to Sultan Rumba. There was no ivory ; their trade was just this *viramba*. And every town was enormously big ; every town was a whole country. So we passed through ever so many districts till we came to Sultan Sangwa, at Mka-suma ; only there he is called Mfisonge.

'There are no native Sultans in these countries, but people come there from far away, who give goods and make payments to those who own the lands and these set up such an one as Sultan for a period of two years. As soon as one has established himself, another comes from far off in the same way, builds himself a house in the forest, and pays goods, stuffs, slaves, goats, beads, and vegetable oil until he who reigned before him has finished his two years and retires. Then the other steps in—such is the custom there—and receives the produce of two years. And likewise in those regions, when anyone dies who is in debt and cannot pay, they do not bury him ; or if he is buried, those who have buried him must pay. He is taken into the forest, and they hang him upon the fork of a tree. Below they place his hoe or his axe or a basket at the place where the dead man is hung up. If anyone

6

comes who has a claim on him, he is told : " If you will have what is yours from yonder debtor, take his axe or his hoe." Such is the nature of their laws and customs.

'And as we marched they committed many acts of violence against us and robbed us ; but we put up with it, for they acted as if we had no weapons, as if we carried rammers. So we marched until one day we found a Shensi who could speak Kirua tolerably. He asked us : " What is really your desire ?" We answered him : " We are looking for ivory." Then he said : " If you want ivory, cross the Lomami, and go to Koto ; there is much ivory there. Or go to Utetera, to Sultan Kassongo Rushie, the son of Mapunga. That is not at all far from here. There is plenty of ivory there. This Kassongo Rushie is very old, and had two sisters, named Kina Daramumba and Kitoto. And a long time ago, as we have heard from our parents, there was a great Sultan in Urua named Kumambe. His second name was Rungu Kabare. He was very powerful, and ruled all Urua as far as Mtoa, and he made war upon all the Manyema lands and the lands on the far side of the Lomami. He came also to Utetera, and carried off the two sisters, Kina Daramumba and Kitoto. They are of the race of the Wana wa Mapunga. There there is very much ivory. And two roads lead thither. One passes through Nsara, and the Sultan is called after the country, Mwinyi Nsara. By this road you will come across Kasongo Rushie, who is on good terms with the people of Nsara. On the second road you will come to Mkahuja. The people there are among

the opponents of Kassongo Rushie—the people
from Nsara and Nguo and Kibumbe and Isiwa, and
Mkatwa and Msangwe—in short, more than twenty
countries with great Sultans, not counting a number
of small Sultans—all these have banded themselves
together to fight against Utetera. And the inhabitants of Utetera are very numerous, but rather
stupid. When they are attacked they become
terrified. Every time they were attacked they
were beaten, and that has made them still more
cowardly." I wrote down all the stories which that
Shensi told me.

'We went on and marched until we came to a
place where we saw that our people had halted;
the road branched off there. And they asked us:
"Where do you want to go?" We said to them:
"We are going to Kassongo Rushie at Utetera."
They replied: "That is this way—take it!" We
marched further and bivouacked in villages. In the
morning we started off again. When it was twelve
o'clock we came to towns of another kind. The inhabited places succeeded one another; they were
not built like those we had come from. They were
built as in Urua—large towns and many in number.
One could see how one town joined another, for the
country is very open. We remained twelve days,
and it rained during that time. They brought us
very much ivory, and it was cheap. For two
vivangwa and a red coral and a garment you
got 2 or 3 *frasilas* of ivory. The tusks had no
value. You gave as much as you wanted to give
and then said: "Off with you quickly!" When
twelve days were past ivory became scarce. Then

came a Shensi who could speak Kirua very well.
He was a great rogue, and was called Pange Bondo.
He brought about four tusks and begged for my
friendship. I said: "Well, you are my friend."
Then he said to me: "I have been Sultan in this
country, and we have the following rule: Out of
those who are born in the sovereignty one line always
comes to power. When one line retires the other
takes its place—and so on, each line in its turn.
Each remains in power for two or three years, and
then withdraws without contention. Then another
succeeds." Pange Bondo, however, refused to
retire when his time was out, and they made war,
and the Sultan whose turn it was next was beaten.
They deposed him and chose another Sultan. And
they said to him: "You will not get the sovereignty
again, even when the Sultans who now precede you
have finished their time, nor will your children ever
succeed, for you have offended against our Constitu-
tion." Then he knew he would not rule again.
When it came to his turn another succeeded to the
throne.

'When we saw that trade fell off and no more
ivory was forthcoming, we determined to go to
Utetera. The Shensis of Mkahuja said to us: "You
must not go to Utetera before having been to
Kirembwe." In the morning we started and proceeded to the frontier of Mkahuja. When we
reached that frontier the Sultan came in the afternoon with about 400 men. They asked us: "Where
are you going?" I answered them: "To Utetera."
Then the Sultan said: "Give me presents, then we
will grant you the permission." We gave him

some twenty garments and ten garments to his men
and about 2 *frasilas* of beads. He said : "It is
well." Just then people came from Kirembwe and
said to us : "You must come to Kirembwe; you
must not go to Utetera. The Watetera, you know,
are subject to us ; we have often marched out and
defeated them. But now we will fight against
them, you and we, and the ivory we will give to you ;
the women we will take ourselves." But we said
to them: " We will only go to Kassongo at Utetera."
We waited till the afternoon, then four Shensis
arrived, who came from Utetera ; they had marched
through the forest and came to our camping-place.
They asked : "Where is Tippoo Tib ?" Then they
were brought to me, and I asked them : "What
do you want ?" They replied : "Kassongo Rushie
sends us. He begs that you will come to him.
There is much ivory there ; what you have bought
comes from us." Then I said to them : "It is well.
Utetera, you must know, is my home. Kassongo is
my grandfather."* They asked : "How so ?" I
told them : " Ages ago there was in Urua a Sultan,
Rungu Kabare Kumambe, who made war on all
countries, and amongst others came against Utetera.
There he took captive two women, Kina Daramumba
and Kitoto, and took them with him to Urua.
There my grandfather, Habib bin Bushir el Wardi,
my mother's father, who had also come to Urua,
met them, and he bought one of the women and
made her his wife. In this way my mother was
born. When I was born she said to me : " In my

---

* Properly ' great-uncle.' The Swahili always has at his
disposal a great number of babas, mamas, and babus.

own country I am a great Princess, and there is very
much ivory there. And our elder brother is called
Kassongo Rushie Mwana Mapunga.' Then I determined to come, and fought with everyone who
came in my way, with the object of reaching my
home." These men were seven in number : four left
us on the spot and three remained with us in fear,
and we concealed them. In the night the drum was
beaten, and the Shensis said : "To-morrow there will
be war."

'In the morning came that Sultan of Mkahuja
with 400 of his people. The place where we had
made our camp was surrounded by towns ; they
were all large places. We had all of us slung
our guns about us, and had small shot and bullets
ready. Then two tusks of ivory were brought us
while we were engaged in fastening up our loads
and packing our tents. The tribesmen who were
with me said : "You go on with the guns ; we who
are behind will conclude the bargain." But I said
to them : "That will not do ; these Shensis have
been beating the war-drum all night, and the people
we have with us, the Watetera, say that we shall
quite certainly be attacked, and the principal chief
of Kirembwe, named Kingoigoi, has barred our
way ; therefore, it is better to conclude the bargain
while we are all together." So we proceeded to
conclude the bargain, and while doing so we were
surrounded by a great crowd of Shensis ; the Sultan
and his people were in the middle of it. But we
had said to our men : "No guns are to be fired
unless someone is attacked, for these folks believe
our guns to be rammers ; it is better that they should

continue to think so." Suddenly we heard the
report of two guns, and at the same time came two
of our Wanyamwezi who had been hit by arrows.
Directly afterwards we saw the Shensis flinging
spears at us. Then we attacked them.'

Of course it was an easy matter to defeat their
wholly untrained hordes. As usual, several towns
were burnt down, and the inhabitants with their
cattle driven off. Their simplicity showed itself
afresh in their begging Tippoo to recall their fallen
countrymen to life. The report of the guns, which
they thought *muhogo* - crushers, seemed to them
thunder. As storms were very common in their
country, they believed that their fallen brethren
had fainted at the sudden claps, and would easily
be waked again with a little *daua* (magic drugs).

Peace was negotiated by Pange Bondo, who stipulated as a main condition that he should be again
set up as Sultan. This was willingly granted him
by Tippoo, but the Mkahuja people, as a counter-
poise, demanded their captured fellow-tribesmen
back. To this, too, Tippoo agreed at the advice
of his friend, for most of the captives were, as was
proved later, not children of the country, but slaves
from Utetera. After the conditions had thus been
agreed to, Pange Bondo was restored to his old
inheritance with great pomp. The coronation was
performed in this way : his subjects clapped moist
clay on his head and strewed flour over it ;
round his neck they hung a chain and ten living
chickens. This ornament he had to wear for ten
days, without regard to the fact that the birds died
off in the meantime. On the handing over of the

prisoners the wily Pange once more showed himself a true friend to Tippoo. The latter naturally did not possess ethnological experience enough to distinguish the people of Mkahuja from the Utetera prisoners, and without the help of the new Sultan would have been badly overreached.

With the mocking humour peculiar to him, the autobiographer recounts in a graphic way how Pange helped him out of his difficulty. One morning the two augurs, followed by a crowd of people, proceeded to a large vacant space where the prisoners of war were marshalled. Tippoo Tib seated himself and took a book in his hand, from the magic formulæ of which, as he informed the wondering assemblage, he would learn which of the prisoners was a native of the country and which a Mtetera.* He made the men march past singly, and with confounding accuracy pronounced the first dozen to be Watetera; the thirteenth was the first of Mkahuja's men. And so it went on, until it turned out that, out of a thousand prisoners, only about a hundred were fellow-tribesmen, who were given back, according to the agreement. The crowd was speechless with consternation at the omniscient stranger, and Pange himself, the old rascal, affected boundless astonishment. He jumped about as if possessed, slapped his legs with his fists, and cried : ' Just look at the sorcerer ! You wanted to fight with a man like that !'

The solution of the riddle was very simple. It

* The prefix *u* signifies the country, the prefix *m* (plural *wa*) its inhabitants ; *ki* at the beginning of a word signifies language, custom, quality.

had been agreed that Pange should make him a
sign every time a fresh prisoner was marched by.
If he cast down his eyes, it was a Mtetera passing ; if
the passer was a man of Mkahuja, the chief looked
up in the air.

The caravan got under way with its new booty,
and after four days' march reached a town called
Msange, on the borders of Utetera. The name
Msange signifies, in the author's opinion, a settlement of men belonging to various tribes who had
joined together here on the frontier to keep off
common enemies. It was thus not a wholly
Watetera town, though these seemed to form the
majority.

After the travellers had made themselves at home
on the camping-ground assigned to them, a relative
of the Sultan, named Ribwe, visited them, who
struck Tippoo Tib by his exceptionally large build.
To him Tippoo Tib again dished up his well-
prepared tissue of lies as to his relationship with
the Sultan, and recounted in a touching way how
year by year, not shrinking from war or privations,
he had journeyed in order to see the relatives of his
much-loved mother.

Ribwe, whom the vast knowledge of the stranger
must have fully convinced, was so touched by this
proof of his kinsman's affection that he at once sent
his new cousin 300 goats and 20 elephants' tusks,
and informed the Sultan, who lived four marches
away, of the joyful discovery. Kassongo, equally
convinced, at once sent envoys to fetch Tippoo Tib.
He did not require much pressing, and hastened
to the capital, which was of moderate size, and

inhabited only by Kassongo and his wives ; it was, however, completely surrounded by larger towns. Kassongo himself, the ruler of an important tract between Lomami and Sankurru, was an old man of eccentric habits. The only beings that he regarded as his social equals were the sun and the elephant. He considered both these as Sultans like himself. He demonstrated his respect for the sun by never looking at the sunrise or the sunset, for he considered it improper to watch the toilet of his royal brother. His regard for his brothers the elephants he displayed by never eating their flesh or touching their tusks.

If one may believe Tippoo Tib, Kassongo voluntarily resigned the sovereignty over the whole country in his favour the very morning after his arrival. Extraordinary as this may seem, yet it appears to have been the truth that our traveller with his clumsy artifice found credence, and at once became ruler of the country. To the simple Shensis, who till then had scarcely come into contact with civilized tribes, it must have seemed inexplicable how a stranger come from afar should on his first entry into the country be acquainted with the whole genealogy of the Sultan's family. Moreover, it stood Tippoo Tib in very good stead that he had had the opportunity at Mkahuja of making prisoners of several hundreds of Watetera. These he brought back to his adopted grandfather as a present, and was thus enabled to show his family feelings in a most disinterested fashion, and so destroy any possible doubt of the genuineness of his blood-relationship. So he became Sultan of

Utetera, in full legal sovereignty. He exercised
justice and exacted heavy penalties from all who
committed offences. He also appointed subordinate
rulers, who had to pay him heavy tributes. Kassongo's conscientious attitude towards the elephants
turned particularly to his advantage. As the succession in the office of ruler did not bind him to
share the scruples of his kinsman, he could take
all the ivory for himself, and if he does not exaggerate, within a fortnight he had acquired 200 tusks,
of a weight of $374\frac{1}{2}$ *frasilas*.

In other respects, too, he did not, in his activity
as Sultan, forget his business as a merchant. He
sent out his uncle Bushir bin Habib to trade in
Ukusu, a district lying to the west. As usual, this
commercial journey degenerated into a plundering
expedition, and Bushir, together with ten Zanzibaris
and fifty Wanyamwezi, paid for the attempt with
their lives. They were one and all devoured by the
cannibal natives. This again was the signal for a
great campaign, conducted by Tippoo Tib himself.
Even old Kassongo would not be held back from
taking part in the expedition. In spite of all representations to the contrary, he insisted on not parting
from his long-lost great-nephew ; after having lost
his two sisters he would not survive their grandson.
If Tippoo Tib was doomed to die now, he would at
least share his fate.

The advance was made with a large force. Tippoo
Tib declares they had in a few days got together
100,000 men. The number is, of course, exaggerated, for the Arab has no conception of exact
computation, besides which he is fond of big-sound-

ing figures. But an imposing levy was no doubt
mustered. Killing and burning, as usual, they
marched from place to place, and the cruelties
elsewhere practised were enhanced by all the male
prisoners being devoured, at which the victors
developed a hearty appetite, two of them eating up
a whole man. Tippoo Tib endeavoured to put a stop
to these doings—less out of love for his neighbour
than because the sickening smell of the slaughtered
human flesh upset him. The Manjema, however,
paid little heed to his representations. ' If,' they
replied, ' we are not to eat men's flesh, do you refrain
from goat's flesh.' In face of this reasonable argument things remained as they were. After two
months the claims of justice were satisfied, the
natives who were left alive paid an indemnity of
sixty tusks as a mark of submission, and the victorious army withdrew.

Tippoo Tib's absence from Utetera had been
utilized by Mkahuja to avenge himself for the defeat
inflicted on him. He had raided a village on the
frontier, plundering in the usual manner. Thus our
hero on returning from one campaign had at once
to undertake another. Old Kassongo again accompanied him. This time it was more serious, for the
enemy was strong, yet he was overcome within forty
days. A large territory was subjugated and much
booty in ivory and goats secured.

The supply of ivory now came in very copiously,
for the conquered districts had to surrender all the
tusks they had. Pange showed himself a very trusty
subject, who paid his tribute regularly.

So Tippoo Tib spent several years occupied with

the duties of a ruler in his own territory and with
expeditions, partly peaceful, partly warlike, into the
country round. In Marera, a district to the east, two
chiefs, Lusuna and Mpiana Nguruwe, vied with each
other for his favour. The first, after having made
various presents of ivory, sent his brother Rumwangwa as a regular envoy. He was received by the
newly installed Sultan with all honour. In the course
of the interview they came to talk of the fact that
Tippoo Tib's guns were greatly damaged and
urgently needed repairs. Then Rumwangwa mentioned that quite close at hand there were countrymen of Tippoo Tib's, who would certainly be able to
repair the damages. Thus our hero learned by
accident that only a few days' march from his place
of sojourn there was a flourishing Arab settlement,
at Nyangwe, on the Congo.

Naturally he at once became anxious to put himself in communication with his fellow-tribesmen who
were so unexpectedly his neighbours, and he set off
for Lusuna's country.

On the way, however, his people broke the peace
by committing various acts of plunder. Lusuna,
out of regard for his powerful ally, winked at the
matter, but managed to induce him for the present
to remain behind with the bulk of his people ; he
himself would take a small body with the damaged
guns to Nyangwe, and so establish communications.

On the way they were attacked and fired upon by
Arabs from Nyangwe, who were just making a raid
into the country round. But when they saw that
they had not to do with enemies, they parleyed with
them and learned that an Arab named Tippoo Tib

wanted to put himself in communication with them. They had often heard the name, but did not know which of their countrymen was the celebrated bearer of that designation. At their request our hero was fetched, and was at once recognised by them as the famous son of old Muhammed from Tabora.

CHAPTER VIII

THE ARAB TOWNS OF NYANGWE AND KASSONGO

' No! here is not any need :
Black the maidens, white the bread !'
GOETHE : *Soldier's Comfort.*

GREAT was the joy of meeting again, especially for
Tippoo Tib, who for almost ten years had been cut
off from intercourse with his brothers and had no
idea how matters stood at home. He learned that
Sultan Majid had died meanwhile (1870), and that
his brother Burghash, Tippoo Tib's enemy, reigned
in his stead. He also heard of the great cyclone
which in 1872 devastated the island of Zanzibar,
tore down houses and uprooted the strongest trees.
So, too, it was interesting news to him that political
conditions had changed considerably in Tabora.
Also they related that a European named Cameron,
with whom we shall have to concern ourselves more
closely directly, had arrived among them.

The leaders of the Arab host were two men of the
coast, Mwinyi Dugumbi and Mtagamoyo. They
wanted to take Tippoo Tib with them at once to
Nyangwe, but he preferred first to settle certain
business in his own country, and for the present
only sent some men with them to supply verbal

proof to the Arab settlement that Hamed bin
Muhammed was identical with the celebrated Tippoo Tib.

After a few days he followed in person. Nyangwe
made on him—accustomed as he had been for years
only to native villages—the impression of a prominent capital. And, in fact, it was the *entrepôt* for the
whole country to a great distance round. It lay, as
Cameron recounts, on a hill that secured it from
fever, and consisted of two different settlements
situated on the right bank of the Congo. The more
easterly, which was kept clean, was inhabited by
Arabs and the better class of Swahilis ; the western-
most was the abode of the ordinary people of the
coast and the Shensis. Their chief was the Mwinyi
Dugumbi aforesaid, whom Cameron describes as a
rascal, ruined by drink and sexual excesses.

The Arabs here formed an imposing community.
Unlike other countries which they only passed
through to plunder, they had established here a
secure fastness, in which they might feel themselves
at home, and safe from any danger of attack. Here,
too, the Arabs' peculiar love for agriculture had
again come to the fore. In the well-watered low-
lands of the river they had laid out broad rice-fields,
which flourished so luxuriantly that people called
the whole country New Bengal. Tippoo Tib and
his people, who for many years had seen no rice,
felt their mouths water when they could once more
enjoy the old familiar dish.

Soon after our hero's arrival at Nyangwe, the
traveller Cameron, who was the first man to
cross the Dark Continent, appeared on the scene.

Originally an English naval officer, he had been chosen in 1872 by the London Geographical Society to go to the assistance of Livingstone. On March 24, 1873, he started, with three European companions, from Bagamoyo. At Unyanyembe he encountered the body of the great explorer, which was being borne to the coast by his faithful servants. One of Cameron's companions undertook the guidance of the convoy; the two others soon succumbed to the effects of the climate. Cameron marched on alone to Ujiji, which he reached on February 24, 1874. Between March 13 and May 9 he passed round Tanganyika, and discovered in doing so the Lukuga, its westerly outlet to the Lualaba. Proceeding further west on May 18, he arrived in August at Nyangwe, where for a fortnight he endeavoured in vain to procure boats to go down the Lualaba. Although he did not as yet suspect that that stream was the Congo itself, he was convinced from the measurements he had taken that it must be one of its principal tributaries, and could not, as was generally believed, belong to the river system of the Nile.

On August 19 Tippoo Tib visited him, and at once, with the chivalry he always showed to European travellers, offered his services for his further journey westwards. He proposed to him to follow him to his camp on the Lomami; from there on he would furnish him with guides, who would be easy to find, as natives in small bodies were constantly in communication with the Sankurru. As it happened, some people from those districts were present and could confirm Tippoo Tib's statements.

7

It must be admitted that the latter's partiality for
the European was regarded with great disfavour by
his compatriots ; but he not only paid no heed to
their representations, but allowed himself to be induced by Cameron, who wanted to lose no more
time, to make a particularly hasty start. His intention had really been to make a trip shortly to the
equally important Arab settlement of Kwa Kassongo,* which lay lower down the river, but he
allowed himself to be turned from his purpose by
the urgent entreaties of his protégé.

On August 26 they set off together, crossed the
Ruvubu, passed through various villages laid waste
by Arab bands ; and though Cameron, owing to
violent attacks of fever, could not make the usual
marches, they arrived by the 29th at a village of
Lusuna's, near which they pitched their camp.
Before this they had had a bloody encounter with
natives, who recognised in some of the people who
had joined the caravan from Nyangwe their old
enemies. The intervention of Tippoo Tib, however,
who was everywhere feared, soon restored peace.

They rested for some days near the village where
Lusuna was staying just then, as Tippoo Tib had
various matters to discuss with his ally. Lusuna
came backwards and forwards on visits to the camp ;
still more often did his wives, whose remarkable
beauty had made a particular impression on the
English traveller. They gradually became very
confiding, and a busy intercourse sprang up between

---

* The place was really called Mwana Mamba, but, because a
Kassongo ruled there, was mostly styled by the Arabs Kwa
(Big) Kassongo, and later simply Kassongo.

the township and the stranger's camp. Lusuna was
in the habit of bringing with him on his visits a
special carved chair, and using the lap of one of his
wives as a footstool.

On their onward march the caravan came to a
township, which was the chief's real capital and
inhabited by him and his wives. Lusuna's marriage
relations were, according to Tippoo Tib's account,
a remarkable freak of polygamy. Of actual wives
he had thirty, who lived with him in his homestead.
The other women inhabitants of the place also
counted as his wives, only they were legally entitled
to provide themselves with other domestic companions. The children born of them were reckoned
in any case as Lusuna's offspring, and might attain
to the throne like his actual offspring. On
September 3 Tippoo Tib's camp was reached. It
was situated very favourably on a low eminence.
In spite of its temporary character, it had pleasant
houses, of which one with two living-rooms and a
bath-room was set apart for the European guest.

Soon after their arrival Kassongo announced his
visit, which was awaited in an open hall built for
gatherings. The Arabs put on their garments of
state in honour of the chief. Cameron as a tattered
traveller could not appear in gala costume. He
dwells on this with regret, and is quite right in his
instinct if he sees a shortcoming in his shabby
clothing. Man in a state of nature makes a great
deal of an imposing exterior, and among the indis-
pensable paraphernalia of an explorer should certainly be numbered a few garments of ceremony.
Zintgraff, the explorer of the Cameroons, after he

had realized this necessity, had a white silk burnous made for state occasions; while Peters, in his Emin Pasha expedition, devised a fancy uniform bedizened with gold in order to impress the Masai.

Cameron's account of his visit is as follows :[*] 'An individual authorized by the chief to do duty as master of the ceremonies then arrived, carrying a long carved walking-stick as a badge of office, his appearance being the signal for all porters and slaves in camp and people from surrounding villages to crowd round to witness the spectacle. The master of the ceremonies drove the anxious sightseers back, and formed a space near the reception-room—as the hut may be termed—and their different subchiefs arrived, each followed by spearmen and shield-bearers, varying in number according to rank, a few of the most important being followed also by drummers.

'Each new-comer was brought to the entrance, where the Arabs and myself had taken our seats, and his name and rank proclaimed by the master of the ceremonies, who further informed him the position he was to occupy in order to be ready to welcome Kassongo. After some time spent in this manner, much drumming and shouting announced the approach of the great man himself. First in the procession were half a dozen drummers; then thirty or forty spearmen, followed by six women carrying shields; and next Kassongo, accompanied by his brothers, eldest son, two of his daughters, and a few officials about him, the rear being brought up by spearmen, drummers, and *marimba*-players.

[*] 'Across Africa,' 1877, vol. ii., p. 21.

On his reaching the entrance to the hut, a ring was formed, and Kassongo—dressed in a jacket and kilt of red and yellow woollen cloth, trimmed with long-haired monkey-skins (a present from Tippoo Tib), and with a greasy handkerchief tied round his head—performed a jigging dance with his two daughters.

' The terpsichorean performance being concluded in about a quarter of an hour, he then entered the hut, and we had a long conversation.'

Cameron informed the chief that he wanted to cross the Lomami and proceed to the Sankurru, which he believed to be a lake, and Kassongo readily offered to help him by negotiations with the Sultan of the territory to be traversed. However, the answer sent back by him was that ' no strangers with guns had ever passed through his country, and that none should do so without fighting their way.'

The European was not disposed to risk forcing his way through, though with Tippoo Tib's help he felt himself strong enough to do so, but luckily it proved possible to reach his goal by a circuitous route. He learned from various quarters that Portuguese traders had arrived at the capital of Urua, to the south-west of his present place of sojourn. As a proof of the truth of this statement, an old Portuguese soldier's coat was shown him, which a native had recently received from one of the white men.

So Cameron determined as his next step to get into touch with these Portuguese, and Tippoo Tib gave him three guides, who journeyed ten days

with him on the road. He reached the capital of
Urua, and found there Portuguese half-castes, who,
although Christians, were carrying on a brisk trade
in slaves. Indeed, they behaved much more cruelly
than their Arab fellow-traders, to whom no religious
injunction of love for one's neighbour forbids this
traffic as sin. After eventful journeys in the southern
districts—which Tippoo Tib had passed through
before—Cameron arrived with his Portuguese companions, more dead than alive, at Benguela, on the
West Coast, in November, 1875, and thus completed
the first crossing of Africa—a meritorious exploit,
rich in geographical results.

After his men returned, Tippoo Tib had waited
three months longer in his camp, so as to be able
to help Cameron in case he came back unsuccessful.
As, however, nothing further was heard of him, he
departed to attend once more to his duties as ruler
and to his business affairs.

To begin with, he wanted to make the journey,
already planned, but given up on Cameron's account,
to Kwa Kassongo, where dwelt many of his friends
from Zanzibar. Above all he looked forward to
meeting again his cousin, Muhammed bin Said—
who died lately at an advanced age in Zanzibar—
known far and wide as Bwana Nzige (Master Locust),
a name given him because his caravans were as
large as swarms of locusts, and ate bare all the
districts that they passed through.

As Kassongo Rushie had abdicated once and for
all, and was glad to have nothing more to do with
the business of government, our hero before leaving
Utetera had to appoint a representative there. He

chose for the post a man of the coast named
Mwinyi Dadi, with whom he left a body of a
hundred Wanyamwezi with fifty guns.

Guided by some of Kassongo's men, Tippoo Tib
first made his way to Nyangwe. The Arabs there
wanted at all costs to induce him to remain with
them, so as to have the support of his powerful
armed force in their constant collisions with the
negro tribes around ; but he would not be persuaded, even when they warned him that there
was famine at Kwa Kassongo. As a born fatalist,
he believed that if he went there Allah, the Lord of
Might, would order all for the best.

At Kwa Kassongo the chief command over all
the Arabs was at once conferred on him. He found
that the people of Nyangwe had only told the truth
about the unfavourable state of things in the place.
Provisions were scarce, and the natives around
showed themselves hostile. The latter fact he had
occasion shortly to experience personally, as 200 of
his slaves were suddenly carried off.

This gave the welcome pretext for a great campaign. True, the Arabs were not well provided
with weapons, but under the leadership of the ever-
victorious Tippoo Tib they feared nothing. The
Shensis were speedily vanquished, and had once
more to pay heavy tribute ; in particular, they were
forced to deliver up all their ivory. After peace
was restored agriculture once more flourished.
There was so much rice that the people of Nyangwe
came over to buy it, and paid a heavy price for it
in ivory. Tribes that lay further away were also
subjugated, so that all the way to Utetera things

were so peaceful that even women could pass to and
fro without risk.

Utetera itself proved to be a regular gold-mine.
Mwinyi Dadi saw to the affairs of his master so
excellently that he could regularly send ample
supplies of ivory.

From Kwa Kassongo Tippoo Tib for the first
time reopened communications with his old father
and other friends at Tabora. Their joy was great
when they heard of the prosperity of the long-
absent one. His messengers found Muhammed
bin Masud, his stepbrother, also at Tabora. Tippoo
Tib, as we know, left him behind at Itahua with
Nsama. After hearing nothing for years of the
brother who had journeyed so far away, he had
returned to the Arab town. During that time he
had acquired 700 *frasilas* of ivory, and passed
them on in Tippoo Tib's name to his creditor, Taria
Topan.

His compatriots at Tabora sent the messengers
back with various gifts, and bade Tippoo Tib come
home as soon as possible. But as trade was just
going well he could not make up his mind to
return, in spite of repeated persuasions. Most of
the Tabora messengers settled down in the new
country, became petty Sultans, and were so pleased
with their position that they never thought of going
home again.

When all messages had thus proved fruitless,
Said bin Ali at last came himself to bring his friend
away. As will be remembered, this Arab had
parted from Tippoo Tib in Urua, in order to trade
in Katanga with Sultan Msire. When his mer-

chandise had come to an end, he had got into communication with Muhammed bin Masud, and proceeded
in company with him to Tabora.

When he now arrived at Kassongo, Tippoo Tib
had just gone down the Congo on a trading trip.
At the news of Said's coming he at once turned
back, and at length allowed himself to be persuaded
to go to Tabora together with his friend. But
before he could carry out this intention fresh warlike occurrences demanded his attention. The
Portuguese traders whom Cameron met in the
south of Urua had invaded Utetera, and robbed and
plundered there. Tippoo Tib marched against them
and defeated them.

On his return to Nyangwe he received the sad
news that his true friend, Said bin Ali, the companion of so many years of wandering, rich alike
in privations and successes, had died. During the
course of the expedition news had been brought that
he had fallen dangerously ill of blood-poisoning.

So the return to Tabora again receded into the
distant future.

CHAPTER IX

WITH STANLEY DOWN THE CONGO

' La abrah hatta ablur magma el baharen au amdhi hukuban.'

' I shall not cease until I reach the junction of the two seas, even if I have to journey for eighty years.'—KORAN : *Suret el Kahaf*, xviii. 62.

SOME months went by in peaceful work at Nyangwe and Kwa Kassongo, when one day the traveller Stanley appeared on his famous journey across Africa. His arrival turned the activity of our hero for the next few months into fresh channels.

Stanley was born, in 1841, in Wales, of humble parentage. His real name was James Rowland, but he was afterwards adopted at New Orleans, where he went as a cabin-boy, by an American merchant and took his name. He travelled as a newspaper correspondent through Turkey, Asia Minor, and Abyssinia. In 1869 Bennett, the proprietor of the *New York Herald*, sent him to Africa to look for the long lost Livingstone. He found him at Ujiji on November 10, 1871. In company with him, he travelled round Lake Tanganyika, and then returned home by Zanzibar, while Livingstone remained at Unyanyembe. This journey had established his reputation as an African explorer. After having taken part in the Ashanti Campaign in 1873-1874, he was secured by the managers of the *New York Herald* and *Daily Telegraph*, who shared the expenses, for a new journey in Africa. Starting from Bagamoyo, he marched, in November, 1874, to the Victoria Nyanza, which he reached in February, 1875. In January, 1876, he visited Mtesa, King of Uganda. That prince placed 2,000 spearmen at his disposal for his further march to Lake Albert. The goal which Stanley reached under this escort was, however, though he was not aware of it, the hitherto undiscovered Lake Albert Edward. From there the explorer turned aside by way of the territory of Karagwe to Tanganyika, which he circumnavigated for the second time, in June and July, 1876. At the end of August he started from Ujiji for the west, and in October reached Kassongo, where, among numerous other Arabs, he found our hero.

The autobiographer describes this first meeting in the following very dramatic fashion :

' At the end of another month Stanley appeared one afternoon. I bade him welcome, and we allotted him a house. Next morning we visited him and he showed us a gun and said : " With this gun you can fire fifteen shots at a time." But we knew nothing of a fifteen-shot gun ; we had neither heard of such a thing nor seen one. I asked him : " From one barrel ?" And he replied : " They come out of one barrel." Then I said to him : " Fire it off, that we may see." But he said : " I will sooner pay twenty or thirty dollars than fire off a single cartridge." Then I thought in my heart : " He is lying. That

is a rifle with one barrel, and the second thing
there must be the ramrod.* How can the bullets
come one after another out of the one barrel ?" And
I told him in turn : " On the Lomami is a bow on
which you place twenty arrows, and when you shoot
it off the whole twenty fly at once, and every arrow
strikes a man."† Then he rose at once, went
outside and fired twelve shots. He also seized a
pistol and let off six shots. After this he came
back and seated himself on the *barasa*. We were
mightily astonished. I begged him " Show me
how you load." Then he showed me.'

Stanley makes no mention of this firing story,
which made such a remarkable impression on
Tippoo Tib, who, like all Arabs, is a great lover
of weapons. But the life-like picture he gives of
our hero is well worth reading.‡

'He was a tall, black-bearded man of negroid
complexion, in the prime of life, straight and quick
in his movements, a picture of energy and strength.
He had a fine, intelligent face, with a nervous
twitching of the eyes, and gleaming white, perfectly formed teeth. He was attended by a large
retinue of young Arabs, who looked up to him as
chief, and a score of Wangwana and Wanyamwezi
followers, whom he had led over thousands of miles
through Africa.

' With the air of a well-bred Arab and almost

* What the narrator takes for the second barrel is the
magazine.

† This answer is quite in keeping with Tippoo Tib's ironical
way. As he thinks Stanley is romancing, he wants to outdo
him by a still bigger lie.

‡ 'Through the Dark Continent,' vol. ii., pp. 95, 96.

courtier-like in his manner, he welcomed me to
Mwana Wambe's village, and, his slaves being
ready at hand with mat and bolster, he reclined
vis-à-vis, while a buzz of admiration of his style was
perceptible from the onlookers.

' After regarding him for a few minutes I came
to the conclusion that this Arab was a remarkable
man, the most remarkable that I had met among
Arabs, Wa-Swahili, and half-castes in Africa. He
was neat in his person: his clothes were of a
spotless white, his fez-cap brand-new, his waist
was encircled by a rich *dowlé* (dagger-belt), his
dagger was splendid with silver filigree, and his
tout ensemble was that of an Arab gentleman in very
comfortable circumstances.'

Stanley's first questions were about the fate of
Cameron, who, aiming at the same goal as himself,
had at this point abandoned the direction he had
kept hitherto and turned off southwards. What
particularly interested him was to learn for what
reasons his predecessor had left the course of the
river.

Tippoo Tib explained this to him clearly and
intelligibly. It was the difficulty in procuring
boats, the threat of hostilities on the part of the
natives of the districts they would have to pass
through, and the disinclination of his own followers
to risk their lives on a river whose channel was
difficult to navigate and whose course was quite
unknown.

With these obstacles, which many years before
had forced Livingstone to turn back, Stanley would
also have to contend. Like Cameron before him,

he endeavoured to secure the powerful assistance of the King of Mamyema, but at first he showed little inclination and excused himself by the fact that at the time he had scarcely 300 warriors with him. These would indeed be enough to go with Stanley, who had a strong force of his own ; but when by-and-by he would have to return without him, he would surely be annihilated. The Shensis, when they saw, as they would, his troops coming back alone and with empty hands, would say that the powerful Tippoo Tib's caravan had been scattered by hostile tribes, and would do their utmost to complete its destruction.

To Stanley's objection that he himself was going to face a still more hazardous future, the Arab coolly rejoined that it was his own personal pleasure if it amused him to risk his life for the discovery of mountains, lakes, and rivers; he himself was a plain ivory-trader, and had no fancy for such unprofitable tricks. At last, however, he went so far as to say that he would sleep over the matter once more.

The next morning, towards eight o'clock, the discussion was continued, and Stanley was requested to set forth his plans more in detail. He replied that he intended to go down-stream in boats until the river took a marked turn either northwards or westwards.

' How far was this by the land route ?'

He did not know ; perhaps Tippoo Tib did.

' No,' replied the latter, ' but I have brought a man with me who has been further down-stream than anyone else.'

The man in question, Abed bin Juma by name, then informed the astonished Stanley that the river flowed northwards and yet further northwards, until at last it emptied itself into the sea. To be sure, he could not say what sea it was ; it could, however, if he was right about it, only be the Mediterranean.

Asked for the source of his knowledge, he told a wonderful story which, although swarming with geographical impossibilities, yet doubtless had a nucleus of truth. It was that on a predatory expedition headed by Mtagamoyo, the fearless leader of the Nyangwe men, after days of marching they had come to the country of the Wakuma, to the west of Lomami. There they had found some representatives of that mysterious race of dwarfs whose existence had long been regarded as a fable, until at length, in 1876, du Chaillu, first among Europeans, found similar pigmies on the Gaboon. The first scientific investigations touching them we owe to Stuhlmann, who in 1893 brought with him to Europe two Batua women from the district west of Ruwenzori. They are scattered from the sources of the Ituri throughout the basin of the Congo as far as the lower course of the Sankurru. They live in groups among the other tribes, with whom they have little intercourse. They inhabit thick forests and live by hunting, which they carry on with poisoned arrows. Their stature never exceeds 4 feet 10 inches, and it is supposed that together with the Bushmen, with whom they have many points of resemblance, they represent the aboriginal race of Africa.

The dwarfs whom the Arabs met said that in
their country there were boundless treasures of
ivory. They themselves attached no value to it,
and even wondered why foreigners wanted it, as
it was not good to eat. Enticed further by these fabulous narratives, Mtagamoyo's caravan after six more
days' march reached the land of the dwarfs proper,
but was very fiercely received by the malicious
little demons. They sprang from the soil around like
mushrooms, and showered their poisoned arrows
on the travellers, causing them endless losses.
Only thirty were able to escape with bare life.
In addition to this, Abed told harrowing stories
of apes as big as men and frightful snakes.

The route by the river was not less dangerous.
Below Nyangwe it was a mass of cataracts, which
would bring certain destruction to any vessel. Old
Daud (Livingstone) had turned back precisely on
this account, and no one would induce the Arabs
to return to those terrible regions.

In spite of this weird description, Stanley, whose
account we are following for the present, persisted
in his plan, and Tippoo Tib showed himself not
averse to it. He first told all the Arabs, with the
exception of his cousin Muhammed bin Said, to
go outside, and then stated his conditions. His
countrymen had indeed urgently dissuaded him
from risking his life, but he did not want to place
Stanley in a dilemma, and so was ready, for a
consideration of 5,000 dollars, to accompany him
sixty days' march, reckoning four hours to each
day.

The following points were agreed upon :

1. The starting-point of the journey to be Nyangwe; the day and the direction taken to be determined by Stanley.

2. The journey not to last longer than three months.

3. The rate of travel to be two days' marching to one day of rest.

4. After Tippoo Tib had accompanied him sixty marches of four hours each, Stanley was to return with him to Nyangwe, unless he met traders from the West Coast on the way, whom he might join and continue his march to the Atlantic. In that case Stanley was to engage himself to hand over two-thirds of his own men to Tippoo Tib as an escort on the return march to Nyangwe.

5. Exclusive of the 5,000 dollars, Stanley was to pay for the keep of 140 of Tippoo Tib's men during their absence from Kassongo, going and returning.

6. If, owing to the difficulties of the country or the attitude of the natives, he should find it impracticable to continue the journey, he would still have to pay the full sum of 5,000 dollars.

7. In case Tippoo Tib should abandon Stanley through faint-heartedness before the expiration of the stipulated time, he was to forfeit all claim to reward or payment for keep.

So far Stanley, from whose statements Tippoo Tib's accounts differ materially. He says that Stanley came to him as a suppliant, and begged and entreated him to accompany him to 'Munza,' a country situated eighty days' march from there in the direction of Mecca—i.e., north-north-east—and he would give him 7,000 dollars (not 5,000); and

8

that no mention was made at that time of the plan of travelling by the river. Tippoo Tib replied that he was not indisposed to come with him, but that he was not doing it out of greed of gold, for he possessed so much ivory that 7,000 dollars were not a consideration to him ; if he went it would principally be out of desire to oblige.

He says that the next morning he declared his readiness to go, but that he did not agree to the conditions recapitulated by Stanley in the manner set forth above ; least of all did any written compact pass between them.

He also emphasizes the fact that his fellow-tribesmen strongly advised him against going, and when they saw he had made up his mind, reproached him violently. He must have gone quite mad, they said, to endanger his life to please an unbeliever. Did he want to become a European himself ? But he answered them with dignity : 'Perhaps I am mad and it is you who are sane. Mind your own concerns.'

It is plain that the accounts are widely divergent. With regard to the sum agreed on—whether 5,000 or 7,000 dollars—perhaps Stanley is the more worthy of credence. The Arab has, as has before been insisted on, little comprehension for figures and loves to exaggerate, while Stanley had no reason to put the amount really promised too low, for he never paid it, as we shall see later on.

However, it is one man's word against another's, and as the negotiation was carried on without the presence of witnesses, it is difficult to decide which of the two accounts is the correct one.

The greater advantage in the alleged compact lay in any case with Stanley. His enterprise would perhaps have been wrecked by the ill-will of the Arab, while the latter would have managed without the 5,000 or 7,000 dollars, and did so manage in the long-run.

Stanley then tells us a pathetic story, embellished with a dramatic night scene, in which he debated with his servant Frank whether they should choose the route which seemed more dangerous, but was more in harmony with the object of their journey along the line of the river, or that which Cameron had adopted through Kassongo's country ; and how they at last decided to settle it by the spin of a coin. A rupee was produced and spun—'head' for the river, 'tail' for the land. 'Tail' came down twice. The straws also, which were next called on for their oracle, gave their voice for the land route. In spite of which the daring travellers decided to follow the course of the river.

After these jests, the description of which displays Stanley's bravado in the proper light, the morning of October 23, 1874, dawned, on which day, according to the English version, the contract was signed and the details agreed to—viz., that Tippoo Tib should take with him on the journey 140 armed and 70 reserve men.

On the 24th they marched from Kassongo to Nyangwe, where Tippoo Tib assembled his men and got them ready for the route. He had in the end, including women and children, a train of 700 souls. Of these, however, 400 belonged to Stanley's following ; the remainder were only to proceed for a few

8—2

days in company with the main body, after which they were to diverge in a north-easterly direction, in order to trade in districts as yet unvisited.

On November 5 the caravan left Nyangwe, and in the afternoon, after journeying a distance of nine and a half miles over a rolling plain covered with grass, reached the villages of Na-Kasimbi, in which they made their first halt. On the 6th they found themselves in face of Mitamba, a thick, black forest, in whose shade, which no ray of sunlight illumined, the travellers were swallowed up. He who has not seen with his own eyes a tropical primeval forest can scarcely form an idea of the horrors of such a wilderness. There is none of the refreshing breath of our native forests ; a stifling, mouldy atmosphere meets the intruder. Between stout and gigantic trees wind creepers as high as a man, which mock the axe as laboriously it seeks to make its way, and grasp with their octopus-like arms at the garments of the wanderer, who worms his way through the less matted spots. The primeval tree-trunks, disturbed in their sleep, shake down their dew in great drops, and the groping foot seeks vainly for a firm hold on the viscous soil.

Stanley was spared none of these difficulties, and his course was still further hampered by the numerous streams, carrying more or less water, that had to be passed. In spite of this, nine to ten miles a day were covered, though the carriers often did not reach the camping-ground till late in the evening. Those among them who had to carry the parts of a steel boat that Stanley took with him fared particularly badly. The sections could not always be

reduced to the dimensions of an average load—
which should not exceed 60 pounds—but had in some
instances to be made into double loads, and in the
closely-tangled undergrowth, through which a single
man could scarcely worm his way, it was a heavy
task to make progress with them. The stipulation
that they were only to march four hours a day soon
fell into disuse over it.

On November 11 the boat-carriers did not reach
camp at all ; they only came in at noon the next day,
completely exhausted.

Of course, under all these adverse conditions,
the mood of the caravan was from the first most
depressed, and degenerated from day to day
into open discontent, the more so as the few who
had followed this route before declared that the
terrors with which they had so far made acquaintance were child's play to what was yet to come.
The most rebellious were naturally the men with the
boat, whose complaints, justified as Stanley could
not but own they were, found a loud echo among
the others.   Even Tippoo Tib sighs at the recollection of the labours of those marches, and among his
followers there was open murmuring, which reached
Stanley's ears, against the ' Forest of the Infidel,' as,
with a certain double meaning directed against the
leader, they christened the jungle they were passing
through.

On November 14 the 300 men of the trading
caravan took leave of them and marched away in a
north-easterly direction.   After a further very trying
march—so Stanley relates—on the morning of the
16th the remainder announced through Tippoo

Tib their determination to turn back. The forest
through which they were now passing was not made
for travel ; only vile pagans, monkeys, and wild
beasts could harbour in it.

After two hours' debate, in which Stanley exerted
all his eloquence, he succeeded apparently in inducing Tippoo Tib to accompany him further. It
was decided to strike off to the river, and march
along its left bank. Tippoo Tib pledged himself,
setting aside the first contract, to twenty more
marches from their present camping-ground, in
return for a wage of 2,600 dollars, and it was decided
to discuss later a possible further extension.

Tippoo Tib's statements here again vary widely
from Stanley's version. He says that the American,
in face of the difficulties of the march and the
unwillingness of the carriers, lost his head completely, and himself made the proposal to diverge to
the Congo. He entirely disputes any reversal of the
compact, to which he had from the first given only a
qualified assent, let alone the lowering of the wage
promised him. However that may be, on November 19 the river was reached, forty-one geographical
miles north of Nyangwe. It was about 1,200 yards
wide, and no longer bore the name Lualaba, as at
Nyangwe. Stanley, not yet knowing that he had to
do with the Congo, called it from this point on the
Livingstone.

After the camp had been pitched they began to
put together the steel boat known as the *Lady
Alice*. Meanwhile Stanley stretched himself in the
grass on the river-bank, and as, full of grave
thoughts, he contemplated the waters flowing past

him into an unknown distance, the resolution ripened
in him at all hazards to navigate their hitherto
uncharted course in boats, regardless whither they
might flow.

At once he summoned his people together in order
to deliver to them a stirring address. To show the
reader how skilful he was in handling the natives,
true to his old journalistic calling, he gives this
speech, which is worthy of embodiment in an epic,
in two pages of print, with all theatrical accessories.
Of course, the effect of his words is that at once half
the at first hesitating blacks swear to follow him
blindly to the death; only Tippoo Tib and a couple of
other Arabs stand aside as an obstinately dissentient
element, and endeavour to dissuade him from his
daring project.

He is already in a fair way to convince these also
by the all-mastering power of his eloquence, when
the palaver is interrupted by the appearance of
several canoes full of natives. Stanley tried, by the
help of an interpreter, to persuade them of his
peaceful intentions; but when they heard that the
new-comers were from Nyangwe, their mistrust was
doubly excited. Even the promise of presents of
untold beads could not induce them to bring their
boats in and take the travellers to the further bank.
On the contrary, they at once raised their war-cry,
which found a hundred echoes in the bushes on the
river-banks.

Meanwhile the steel boat had been put together,
and Stanley crossed to the left bank to open relations in person. The Shensis at length declared
themselves willing to enter into friendly intercourse

with the new-comers, on condition that the white man
should contract blood-brotherhood with their chieftain. An island in the middle of the river was
fixed on as the scene of the solemnity, the time to be
next morning.

Such proposals of fraternization on the part of
natives for the most part amount to a clumsy snare.
This Stanley suspected, so as a precaution he landed
a considerable body of men on the island during the
night. His servant Frank was sent as white man
for the completion of the ceremony, while he himself
remained hard by with the boat, to be ready at once
in case of treachery.

He was not deceived in his forebodings. From
the first the Shensis adopted a threatening attitude,
and soon proceeded to open hostilities. But when
they were confronted by the reserves that had
been concealed during the night, they hastily took
to flight and paddled back to the left bank.

After the failure of this attempt at peaceful relations, Stanley determined at all hazards to transfer
his caravan to the west bank. As many men as the
Lady Alice would carry, thirty in round numbers,
were taken across to begin with; while they set to
work to entrench a camp, the remaining carriers
were gradually fetched, and at length several
Shensis were induced by a bribe of beads to place
six boats at their disposal for transport purposes.
By night on November 20 Stanley's whole caravan
was encamped on the left bank.

By the next morning the hard-won friendship of
the natives was again at an end; all the villages far
and wide were deserted, and so it remained for the
most part during the ensuing march.

Stanley, with a few men, proceeded down-stream in the *Lady Alice*; the main body followed by the land route. Both parties had unpleasant experiences in the shape of hostilities on the part of the dwellers on the banks, but the land detachment came off worse, as it lost its way and had to sustain an engagement with the Bakusu, with much loss. Not till November 26 did the two parties effect a junction, after which they kept more in touch.

In course of time they succeeded in getting together a certain number of native boats, which were very serviceable, as small-pox and dysentery broke out in the land division, and made many men unfit for marching. A floating hospital was formed for them.

The two accounts again differ greatly as to the way in which the boats were procured. Tippoo Tib, who is generally inclined to excuse his sins on the ground of necessity, declares with praiseworthy candour that the canoes were captured in a boisterous ' drive.' He writes :

' I attacked the Shensis, and took their boats and goats from them. Every day I got six or seven canoes, and any number of goats. But the inhabitants are very well trained in making off with their boats. They have also war-drums, called *mingungu*. The first town beats them, then the second follows suit, and every town that hears the signal passes it on. Thus one may travel for two months without finding any people in the townships. You only see goats, for there are very many of them, and they cannot get away. And most of the boats are small, and one does not easily get them unless the occupants hear bullets flying about their ears or

are actually hit by them. Then they plunge into
the water and leave the boats behind them.'

It is easy for Tippoo Tib to be outspoken over this
episode, for he knows that the European reader is
bound to lay the responsibility on Stanley. The
latter, however, in full consciousness of innocence,
disdains to invoke the plea of necessity, well-
grounded though it was, and describes to us how he
obtained lawful possession of the boats in a perfectly
peaceable manner. In the first instance six master-
less canoes were found and appropriated, while on
December 4 they discovered a very large boat that
had clearly been abandoned for years ; this, though
much damaged, was also annexed, and, after the most
urgent defects had been repaired, could carry sixty
persons.

These pieces of luck of course materially facili-
tated their advance, but for all that there were
difficulties enough, while sickness and the hostility
of the natives gave them no respite. More lives
were lost daily. On the 11th eight corpses, among
them the three youthful favourites of our hero,
were sunk in the waters of the fatal stream. In
the middle of December the river wing had a serious
encounter near the village of Vinya Nyaza, which
might easily have been fatal, but was turned into a
victory by the timely arrival of the land wing.
The Shensis took to flight, and in pursuing them
thirty-eight canoes, mostly quite good ones, were
taken.

On December 22 formal peace was concluded,
and the long-desired blood-brotherhood accomplished. The Shensis received back twenty-five
boats ; the remainder were retained as a suitable

indemnity. Stanley was now sufficiently provided
with boats to dispense with further help from
Tippoo Tib. They agreed to part here, somewhat
above the mouth of the Kasuku.

As to the manner of their agreement the accounts
again differ fundamentally. Stanley declares that
Tippoo Tib expressed to him so categorically his
intention of turning back at this point that he
abandoned all attempts at talking him over, although,
according to the last compact, the Arab chief was
still bound for eight days' march.

The latter, on the contrary, asserts that Stanley,
after thanking him heartily for the support so far
accorded him, himself suggested his return, as he
had boats enough to proceed alone. All he had
stipulated with him was that Tippoo Tib should steal
two larger boats, in which he could conveniently
ship his riding asses ; and this *coup* they had
carried out together with great success.

On one point the two narrators agree—that the
condition was made that Tippoo Tib should exert
his influence to induce Stanley's men under all
circumstances to continue the march. Stanley is
silent as to how this influence was brought to bear,
while our autobiographer gives the following
delightful description :

'Hereupon Stanley summoned his men and said
to them : " Hamed bin Muhammed will turn back at
this point. But do you make ready. The day after
to-morrow we shall start." Then the men answered
him : " If Hamed bin Muhammed turns back, we
shall all turn back. We are not going into unknown regions. We engaged on the coast for two
years, and now it is two years and a half. If Hamed

bin Muhammed turns back, we shall certainly turn back too." And all the men persisted obstinately that they would not go further. Then Stanley became very mournful ; even his food was no longer tasteful to him, and he was on the point of weeping.

'In the evening he came to me and said : " My whole labour is lost if these men turn back. Then I too must turn back, and my toil has been in vain, Help me now, I implore you." I said to him : " God willing, I will help you under all circumstances !"

'I lay down to sleep, and next morning visited him and asked : " What have you decided ?" He replied : "I have decided nothing, and I don't know what I am to do." Then I said to him : " Well now, follow my advice. Assemble all your people, then call me and speak to me with harsh words, and say : " If you go back all my people will turn back. They cannot do otherwise. Now, my work is for the State, and that is no other than Seyyid Burghash. If my people turn back, I must turn back too. Then I shall tell the Sultan that it was Hamed bin Muhammed who made my further journey impossible. Then the State will confiscate your goods. When you have said that it is well, then I shall speak." Then I went away.

'In the afternoon he sent for me and called together his people, and spoke to me in presence of his men in harsh words, as I had prompted him. Thereupon I said to them: "You have heard Stanley's words ; now get you on your way and depart. Whoever follows me I will kill ; for you would plunge me in ruin and my property would be confiscated by the Government. Then I should be as good as

dead. My toil during many years would be in vain.
Should I not certainly perish here ? If you follow
me, I will kill you." Thereupon I withdrew and
they went their way.

'Towards evening came Stanley's people, and
their leaders said to me : " Our time with this
European is over ; we positively must turn back."
I said to them : " Your words are idle—march on."
Then said they : " Do you wish us to perish ?" I
answered them : " As it is with him so it will be with
you. If you are lost you will be lost together." Then
they said : " This European is a churl. He gives
us nothing without putting it down—not even
clothes does he give us ; not a single loin-cloth does
he give." I said to them : " Let that be my care. I
will give you as much as you want. Only go on."
Then they answered me : " What, then, are we to
do ? We are now afraid of you, because of the
words you have spoken. But with this European
we have nothing to do. Our time was up more than
six months ago." But I said to them : " Your
words are idle. Do as I tell you." '

Then, according to Tippoo Tib's autobiography,
Stanley at his instance gave his men nine loads
of garments, and thus won them, by gentle compulsion, to accompany him further.

Although Stanley leaves these small details
unmentioned, he describes all the more minutely
the rewards which he bestowed on Tippoo Tib and
his men. Thus our hero received a voucher for
2,600 dollars, a riding ass, a chest, a gold chain, a
revolver, ammunition, and great store of beads,
copper wire, and clothes. His followers, according

to their rank, received from 1 to 20 *dotis* of material
for clothing.

Tippoo Tib in his autobiography says not a
word of these presents of Stanley's, though he
admitted to the author verbally that he received a
draft for money, but the amount was not communicated to him, and as he cannot read English he
could not learn what it was. He sent the cheque
to his business friend Taria Topan to be cashed, and
was highly astonished to receive only 2,000—
3,000 dollars on it, instead of the expected 7,000.
He disputes having received the presents enume-
rated by Stanley ; only as regards the donkey, he
does admit that he received two. Stanley had,
it seems, four riding asses, of which he took the
two best with him. He could not ship the other
two, and so gave them away. The stuffs that
Stanley enumerates as presented to him and his
men were really so given, but were not gratuitous.
They represented the payment of the keep, which,
according to compact, Stanley was to supply for the
return of the escort. But he had indeed made him
lying promises, and said :

' I do not know how I can possibly repay your
goodness, nor do I know what I am to give you
in money. For when I return to Europe I shall
receive high honours and much money. I will
present you with a watch worth 1,000 dollars,
with diamonds, and how much money I shall give
you I cannot reckon.'

Finally Stanley begged him to wait for a month
where he was, to be at hand with help in case he
should be forced to turn back.

The last two days chanced to be Christmastide, and were devoted to harmless amusements, so as to distract Stanley's band from the feelings incident to parting, and drive away the cares arising from an uncertain future. The captured canoes received the proud titles of English war-ships, and raced against each other, the winning crew receiving prizes. Foot races also were held, and even the stately Tippoo Tib did not disdain to take part in the sport. The village street, 300 yards in length, was made into a course, on which the Arab chieftain and Frank the servant tested their swiftness of foot. Tippoo Tib was first at the winning-post with a lead of 15 yards, and received a prize of a silver drinking-cup. Races between lads, and even dusky ladies, formed further items in the enlivening programme. A war-dance by the Wanyamwezi, whose deep-toned drums and shrill fifes sent a strange Christmas music into the stillness of the primeval forest, wound up the festal day.

On the second day of holiday-making Tippoo Tib gave a banquet to the whole caravan.

The rice and roast mutton were freely washed down with palm wine, in the forbidden fire of which the last cares for the future were drowned.

On December 27, 1876, Stanley with his following began the further march into the unknown, and at the beginning of August, 1877, reached the West Coast. The principal result of his crossing of Africa, rich as it was in other respects, was that it decided beyond dispute the question of the source of the Congo.

CHAPTER X

'I had no more than this staff when I passed over this Jordan; and now I am two hosts.'—GEN. xxxii. 10.

TIPPOO TIB waited for a month, according to his promise, at the place where Stanley had parted with him, and then marched to the lower Lomami, where he found very advantageous trading conditions.

The natives of those parts had, indeed, no conception that ivory was an object of value. They hunted elephants, it is true, but only for the sake of their flesh; the tusks were for the most part heedlessly thrown away into the bush, where they rotted or were devoured by insects. Here and there the Shensis took them, and turned them to strange uses in the villages. Artists who had a glimmering of the high value of this important product fashioned flutes and household utensils out of it; ivory mortars were common, in which bananas, a leading article of food of these tribes, were mashed up. It was also a favourite plan to plant the tusks in the ground as a fence round the homestead. One can fancy how the Arabs' hearts beat high when they passed such a precious fencing.

As an equivalent for the ivory, copper was given,

which Tippoo Tib had acquired by barter at Utetera. He had bought 5 *frasilas* of that metal there for a *frasila* of beads. Half a *frasila* he had presented to Stanley at parting; for the remainder he now obtained 200 *frasilas* of ivory. A *frasila* of beads cost at the time he purchased it in Zanzibar 3 dollars, while he could sell that weight of ivory for at least 50 dollars. So his 3 dollars had turned into 10,000.

The departure entailed many fresh combats, and the caravan had often to suffer from the poisoned arrows of the Shensis, although there were not so many fatal wounds as before, for the men had learned from Stanley that the wounds must be at once cauterized to avoid the effect of the poison.

Only when the camp was pitched in the immediate neighbourhood of the river had they any peace, for the dwellers on the banks had a lively recollection of the former encounters, and fled hastily to the islands when the travellers came near.

At Kassongo Tippoo Tib found the situation most favourable, and, what was most important for him, the tributes of ivory from the conquered districts had flowed in abundantly. By his subjects he was received with jubilation; they had been distressed at his lengthy absence, and now the news spread like wild-fire through his whole domain that he had come back safe and sound.

As to the two next years, he has not much to record: they went by monotonously with expeditions —some peaceful, some warlike—in the country. He appointed his cousin Muhammed bin Said, who had grown tired of the nomad life, regent in Utetera,

9

where he was so much at ease that he could not wish for anything better ; ' for the Shensis of those regions are good-hearted, the women are fair, and the country is fruitful.'

In the middle of 1879 our hero was again re-minded of his home by messengers from Zanzibar. Sultan Burghash sent him by letter a summons to return at once, as his banker, Taria Topan, wished to settle accounts with him. The two years for which the advances were made had by now grown to twelve, and his business friend must be kept waiting no longer.

In order to give this missive, which was couched in very friendly terms, quite an official character, the Sultan sent with it a valuable present—a modern repeating rifle. The gift was all the more flattering as Tippoo Tib had not as yet had the honour of making the giver's acquaintance. Taria, who also gave him a rifle, wrote in the same strain as the Sultan, and added the news that Stanley had some time before (November 26, 1877) returned to Zanzi-bar, and had said a great deal about his friend Tippoo Tib. There was a letter from him, too, and in it, as a valuable remembrance, Stanley's photograph. At the sight of it our chronicler could not restrain a mocking laugh.

If there is anything for which the Arab or Swahili has by nature no appreciation, it is photographs. If his sight has not been trained by repeated trials to do so, he is quite unable to distinguish the person represented, however well known to him. Now that modern civilization has, among other important necessaries, introduced half a dozen photographers

into the country, every native can acquire this
faculty by staring at show-cases, and he even thinks
it well worth while, if he can muster up the cost, to
rescue his more or less handsome features from
oblivion by having them imprinted on the dark
plate.   But that Tippoo Tib, who in a rough nomad
existence of twelve years had become a stranger
even to the modest luxury of Zanzibar, should have
the very slightest appreciation for the delicate attention of his Western friend, no sensible man could
expect.

So he only felt surprised, and supposed when
Stanley got home he would discharge the remainder of his debt and send the valuable presents
promised.

After Tippoo Tib had received these messages
he needed a whole year to settle all his affairs in
the country.   As he expected to be away for a long
time, he had to take care to fill the important posts
with trustworthy men who combined prudence and
energy with good will, and thus could well watch
over his interests.   In particular Nyongo Luteta,
to whom he entrusted his affairs in Utetera, proved
himself a very useful representative.

At last he set out, in company with his cousin
Bwana Nzige.   Large as was the host of carriers he
took with him, it was not sufficient for the rapid
transport of the boundless stores of ivory which he
had been gathering together for years.   Hence the
following order of march was adopted : Tippoo Tib
went on ahead with the body of carriers, who took
with them as many loads as they could possibly
manage.   After four hours' march he pitched his

9—2

camp and sent the carriers back to his cousin, who remained behind with the unconveyed ivory. When the remainder reached Tippoo Tib's camp next morning, he proceeded further in the same manner. As the distance had thus to be traversed by the carriers three times, of course much time was lost, and the march from Utetera to Tanganyika, which without burdens can at a pinch be made in a month, occupied half a year.

Lake Tanganyika had been since the far-off time when our traveller had last crossed it the goal of many African explorers, and had by their zeal been brought to the closer knowledge of the West. In February, 1858, the English travellers Speke and Burton were the first Europeans to sight the great inland sea; but the first Westerners to navigate it were Stanley and Livingstone, in 1872, after the successful search for the latter in the interior of the Dark Continent. Four years later it was systematically circumnavigated by Stanley in the course of the crossing of Africa which we have described. Much had also been contributed to the exploration of the great sheet of water in 1873 by Cameron, and later on, between 1878 and 1880, by the travellers Hore, Thomson and Cambier, Böhm and Reichhardt.

Tippoo Tib struck the lake at the port of Mtoa, which was known to him of old and used by all the caravans that trafficked with the West. By the busy stir which he found here he could judge how long he had been a stranger to the Eastern world. Where formerly only primitive dug-outs rocked on the waves, stately vessels, such as are to be seen in the Indian Ocean, now proudly spread their sails

to the wind. Even some representatives of the
Western lands, where thirty years before the very
existence of the inland sea had been a fable, had
established a permanent camp here in the heart of
the Dark Continent. Close beside the Arab town
from which the caravans started for the West on
their man-destroying traffic, the English mission-
station of Plymouth Rock looked out on the country
from a low hill, like a bulwark of peace and herald
of a new civilization. The manager of the station,
Mr. Griffith, gave a friendly greeting to the Arab
prince, who was probably well known to him by the
accounts of returning caravans.

On the eastern shore, opposite Mtoa, and in good
weather only one day's sail from it, lies the well-
known Arab town of Ujiji. Here it was, as we have
already seen, that on November 10, 1871, Stanley
found Livingstone. He describes the Arab settlement as a flourishing commercial town, in the much-
frequented market of which the tribes of the
whole interior of Africa fixed their rendezvous.
Wissmann, who in 1882 passed through it soon
after our traveller, found that the town had fallen
off greatly since Stanley's visit. Many houses stood
empty, and their state of disrepair proclaimed that
they had long been uninhabited. The population
was composed partly of Arabs, with their numerous slaves, partly of free natives of the country.
The Wajiji were exceedingly skilful navigators,
and as such were much employed by the Arabs.

Though the latter formed the ruling class, the
real autocrat of the town was a Swahili named
Mwinyi Heri. He had been appointed governor by

Seyyid Burghash, and, as the symbol of his power, proudly hoisted over his hut the red flag of the Sultan.

Ujiji was, however, still an important *entrepôt*, where the products of the country were daily displayed for sale in large quantities, beside the wares of their native Zanzibar — fish, fruit, salt, butter, honey, slaves, ivory and cattle on the one side ; on the other, samples of the wares that were brought by European ships to the shops of the Indians of Zanzibar. Glass beads, red or blue, were in use as payment for the humbler articles.

As a port Ujiji was not well chosen, as the shore is flat and unprotected, so that vessels have constantly to be drawn high and dry. At Wissmann's coming some forty dhows lay in the roadstead—a number never reached at a single port on the coast of German East Africa.

Tippoo Tib halted for the present at Mtoa, but sent his cousin on to greet the Arabs living at Ujiji, to obtain water carriage, and to inquire into the possibility of continuing the march to Tabora. The country was, it must be said, in the highest degree unsafe for caravans, for a powerful native prince named Mirambo had for many years carried on a war of extermination with the Arabs.

We will pause for a moment to consider this interesting personality.

Mirambo was born about 1830 in Unyamwezi, where his grandfather, Mvura, was set up as Sultan of the small and poor district of Ugoa by Tippoo Tib's grandfather, Juma bin Rajab. After Mvura's death an uncle of Mirambo's succeeded to the sultanate, while he himself was left to earn his living unaided ; and in spite of his high family connections he adopted, like most of his compatriots, the calling, more lucrative than princely, of a *mpagasi* (carrier).

On the death of his uncle he became Sultan. He soon extended widely the borders of his hitherto insignificant dominion. With the help of the freebooting Wangoni he first conquered the neighbouring country of Uriankuru, which, together with Ujoa, he united in the sultanate called after him Urambo. By the plundering of many Arab caravans numerous rifles fell into his hands, with the aid of which he extended his influence westward almost to Tanganyika, northwards to the Victoria Nyanza, and southwards to the sixth degree of latitude. His successes made such an impression that supernatural powers were everywhere attributed to him. It was said that he could fly, was invulnerable, and needed no sleep.

With the Arabs of Tabora he was at first on fairly peaceable terms. They reluctantly paid the *hongo* imposed on their caravans, and did not venture in their constant state of disunion to attempt anything against so dangerous a chieftain. At last, however, his encroachments seem to have grown excessive, and in the summer of 1871 it came to a sanguinary encounter between the two parties. Stanley* was just at that time the guest of the Arabs at Tabora, and took part in the conflict. He assigns as the cause of the war that Mirambo had demanded of a caravan marching to Ujiji

* *Cf.* 'How I found Livingstone,' chap. viii.

an exceptionally high toll, and because difficulties were made about the payment, which was, however, at last made, he forbade all Safaris whatever to pass through his territories for the future. Tippoo Tib declares that the quarrel broke out because Mirambo refused to hand over 200 slaves of the Arabs who had fled to his country.

At any rate, when Stanley arrived at Tabora the fury of the Arabs was boundless. The general anger was especially fanned by Khamis bin Abdullah el Barwani, an influential man who, in the course of long journeys, had grown used to bloody conflicts, and regarded it as a disgrace that his fellow-tribesmen there, among whom he had for some time made his home, allowed themselves to be so terrorized by a mere unbeliever.

After long deliberation, a force of 2,255 men, with 1,500 muskets, took the field against Mirambo in the beginning of August, confident of victory. At the end of a week they returned to Tabora in wild flight. Mirambo had fallen on one of the divisions marching against him on the frontier of Uriankuru in the high grass, and destroyed it almost to a man. At the news of this disaster the remaining heroes also turned tail.

On the 22nd of the month Mirambo appeared in person before Tabora. Khamis bin Abdullah, the one brave man among the Arabs, went out against him ; but his little force was surrounded by the superior forces of the savages and annihilated. Mirambo then stormed some of the less well fortified *tembes*, burned down several houses, and looted a quantity of cattle and 200 elephant's

tusks. Then he returned, well satisfied, to his own
territory.

Since that time a regular guerilla warfare had
been carried on between Mirambo and the Arabs.
They had done each other as much damage as
possible by plundering, as occasion presented itself;
but the Arabs suffered the most, as their caravans
could only get to the lake in fear and trembling by
secret paths.

At the end of a fortnight Bwana Nzige returned
with the news that the road to Tabora was difficult
of passage owing to the enmity with Mirambo; but
his compatriots at Ujiji begged Tippoo Tib to
come to them as soon as possible, to talk over in
person the details of the further march. Tippoo
Tib determined to venture on the journey at all
hazards. He intended to leave behind the greater
portion of his ivory and take with him principally
armed men, under whose protection he hoped to
convey safely some 100 *frasilas*. From Tabora
he would then send fresh armed bands to Ujiji to
fetch the ivory left behind without risk.

At Ujiji he had intended to stay with the
Vali, Mwinyi Heri; but an Arab named Muhammed bin Khalfan invited him to come to him,
and Tippoo Tib, after assuring himself that the
chief official of the town would not take it ill,
accepted the invitation. This meeting with his as
yet unknown compatriot was destined to have
disastrous results to our hero, as the subsequent
history will show. Rumalisa—such is the widely
familiar sobriquet of his new friend—robbed Tippoo
Tib of a large portion of his fortune.

Soon after the arrival at Ujiji fresh intelligence came from Tabora to the effect that the road was now quiet. Tippoo Tib thereupon altered his plan so as to take the whole of the ivory with him, and make for his father's town by the nearest way, viâ Ruanda and Uvinza. He was joined by the Arab Salum bin Abdullah el Marhubi, who had been appointed by the Sultan administrator of the inheritance of Said bin Ali, who had died at Kassongo, and accordingly the far from inconsiderable stores of ivory of his friend had been handed over to him at Ujiji. Less than a day's march from that place our travellers found themselves already exposed to various hostilities on the part of the Waruanda. Salum, who had lagged somewhat behind with his men, was surprised by the Shensis and completely stripped. He with difficulty saved his bare life, and reached the camp late in the evening, in rags and bespattered with filth. Two of Tippoo Tib's men, who had ventured some way from the camp to fetch wood, were also killed. Next morning the natives ventured an open attack, but were repulsed.

Then Tippoo Tib assumed the offensive. He constructed an entrenched camp, from which he made raids into the surrounding country. The very first day he had asked support of his countrymen at Ujiji, which soon arrived. With their assistance the whole country was soon devastated, and made so subject to the control of our hero that he was able to regard himself as at home and send for the whole of his ivory. After the lapse of some months his eldest son, Sef, visited him. He had been left behind as a small boy at Zanzibar, where he was brought up. Now he was eighteen years old, and had joined some business friends of his father's—the Arabs Salum bin Omar el Wardi and Said bin Habib el Afifi—on their first trading trip into the interior. He brought a great number of Wanyamwezi with him, who were very welcome to Tippoo Tib as carriers and enabled him to convey a large portion of his ivory.

His fellow-tribesmen at Ujiji viewed his departure with regret. They had taken a delight in the expeditions under Tippoo Tib's ever-victorious leadership, and were afraid that without the prestige of his dreaded name they would not be a match for the numerous Shensis. At their request he left them 140 guns, with the corresponding number of warriors, by means of whom Rumalisa and Mwinyi Heri reckoned on holding in awe Ruanda and Uvinza. Tippoo Tib, however, did this unwillingly, and seems not to have approved of the plans for further fighting. 'These people must always be making war,' he writes in reprobation.

His way through Uvinza was not a path of roses. The ruler there was the powerful Sultan Kasanura, who exacted heavy tolls from travellers. Besides, he carried off all the slaves he could lay hand on, and carriers who ventured away from the camp were inexorably killed.

Our hero would gladly have had recourse to arms in face of these outrages, but prudence restrained him, as he had a large train of carriers and but few fighting men, and defeat would have been likely and the loss of ivory irreparable. Postponing his plans of revenge to a future date, he put up with all these arbitrary acts, and at length, though heavily fleeced, reached Tabora in safety.

He halted at Itura, his wonted quarters. There, after long years, he saw his old father once more, and his step-brother, Muhammed bin Masud, happened to be there also. 'The dancing, the killing of cattle, and the feasting lasted a fortnight. The merriment was extraordinary.

From Tabora Tippoo Tib at once placed himself in communication again with the Sultan and his banker. In order to enable him to provide for the safe transport of his unconveyed ivory, he begged the former to send him a large quantity of powder. The answer came by return that the Sultan had pleasure in presenting him with twenty hundredweight, which would reach him through the agency of Taria Topan.

As our hero, delighted at this prospect, was just about to return to Tanganyika, there came an embassy from the dreaded Mirambo to old Muhammed bin Juma with offers of peace. He appealed to the fact that there had never been enmity between them. On the contrary, since the time of their fathers they had been united in the bonds of friendship. He, Mirambo, respected Muhammed as a father, as he had shown often enough. He had always given Muhammed credit for equally friendly sentiments, though he naturally could not give expression to them out of regard for the other Arabs, Mirambo's sworn enemies. Now he had heard that the son of his friend had difficulties with regard to the ivory left behind on Tanganyika. He, Mirambo, would certainly put no hindrances in his way, and begged him to pass through his territory without fear. He was delighted to make the acquaintance of the far-travelled caravan leader.

Tippoo Tib eagerly took advantage of this favourable disposition, and sent off messengers at once to assure Mirambo of his friendship. On reaching his town, however, they did not find the chief himself there—he had just started on a fresh expedition against the Sultan of Tabora. His brother, Mpanda Sharo, who had remained behind, received the envoys with all honour, and dismissed them with valuable presents.

. The news that Mirambo was again on the warpath soon reached the Arabs at Tabora, but they did not know against whom he was marching, and racked their brains as to the object of his new hostilities.

Tippoo Tib meanwhile had departed westwards. On the frontier of the Tabora territory messengers from his compatriots reached him warning him to go no further, as he might any moment happen upon Mirambo's bands. It was the ninth of the month El Hadj, the eve of the great Arab feast, which he, like all his countrymen, was in the habit of celebrating with great scrupulosity even in the most difficult situations. He replied quite calmly :

' To-day is the ninth of the month ; to-morrow is the tenth of the month El Hadj. As soon as the feast has been kept I shall set out, and all things are in the hand of God, the Lord of Might. I cannot stay. It would cost me much money, and the carriers would also make difficulties for me, in order to get home again.'

In accordance with this programme, he started off after the feast, and encamped near the sources of the Wataturu, one of the few watering-places on this route, visited by every traveller. Here people were wont to provide themselves with the precious fluid sufficiently for the next few days, which led through districts where water was scarce. In the night a heavy torrent of rain broke over them quite unexpectedly, as it was the dry season. All the guns were wet, and there was reason to fear that the powder in them had become useless, so it was proposed to discharge them all and load afresh.

A tremendous volley rang out from 500 muskets, which thundered far and wide through the wilderness, and was heard by Mirambo's men, who were just marching towards the celebrated watering-place. He was returning from a successful expedition, and had no idea that Tippoo Tib was near at hand. Nevertheless, he called out at once when he heard the thunder of innumerable guns: 'That must be Hamed bin Muhammed. No one can shoot like him.' In the hope that Tippoo Tib's route would lead him past his camping-place, he remained there a day longer.

Tippoo Tib, however, had as yet no news of the peaceful result of his mission, and therefore thought it more advisable to avoid for the present a meeting with the powerful chief. Continuing his march at greater speed, he came on many traces of Mirambo's column, and was therefore forced to take special precautions in advancing. Suddenly a fusillade was heard from the rear-guard. Two men were hit by bullets, and in the general confusion various loads went astray. As it turned out later, this was not a deliberate attack by Mirambo, but some of his men who had left the column to plunder had made a marauding attack on their own account, without knowing that the object of it was their master's friend Tippoo Tib.

After a few further marches Tippoo Tib reached Uvinza, where he now intended to take his revenge for the injury done him when marching through. He had beforehand warned Rumalisa to be ready to support him. How he settled accounts with his old enemy Kasanura we can learn best from his own narrative :

'We determined to declare war and smite the Sultan of Uvinza, Kasanura. He had settled on a river. There are five or six ditches there—half on one side and the other half on the other. His town is laid out exactly in the middle. It was strongly fortified and surrounded by a moat. Behind the first entrenchment a second was built, and inside long tree-trunks were planted. The intervening space between the entrenchments was filled up with sand, so that no bullets could penetrate. Towers with loopholes were also built. There was no point open to attack. But we did not know that the city was like that, and sent out men to attack it. They marched there, and passed the first and the second and the third ditch. The water rose to their belts or a trifle higher. When they advanced towards the *boma* the Wavinza in it remained quiet, but when they came quite near they were fired on with small shot, and the enemy sallied out and they were driven back, and many were killed. We asked those that

came back : " How are things there?"   They replied :
" We have come back again, though you could
hardly have hoped for it.   The rest have all fallen."
They came back in twos and threes, and by the evening forty-six men were missing who had fallen.
Their guns were lost, and some even that escaped
had thrown theirs away, to the number of thirty.

'We waited two days, and on the third I determined to start—ourselves, and our belongings, and
our wives.   We marched as far as the river and
there pitched our tents.   Next morning we passed
the ditches, and they sallied out, and it came to a
furious encounter between us, and they fell back to
their fastness.   Next day we crossed with our packs
and our followers, and traversed all three ditches.
Then we pitched our tents, but our camp
had no entrenchment.   They sallied out several
times, but we drove them back, and they fled to
their *boma*.   Each time several men fell, both on
their side and on our side.   So we remained for
several days, but their *boma* was not to be got at on
account of its many defences.

'And they sent out men secretly to beg support
of Mirambo, but he refused, saying : " Hamed bin
Muhammed is my friend.   I cannot help you."   And
he informed me of this.   So a month and a half
passed by, and the struggle became still more furious,
but there was no getting at their *boma*.   Muhammed
bin Khalfan said to me : " Shall we not go into
the moat and fight with them ?"   I answered him :
" You understand nothing of war.   You have never
fought.   He who goes into the moat does not come
out again.   It becomes his grave, and the attack is

foiled." And I had a number of workmen with me
—carpenters—to whom I said : "Make planks ready
for me, but they must be of heavy wood." They
went away and sent across ten boats, which were
very large and of heavy timber. They dragged
them to the spot and broke them up. So we got
long planks. These planks we nailed together and
made wheels underneath. Then we took this
framework to the ditch and set up other planks on
the top, so that those in the towers should not see
the men inside the structure, and when they fired
the bullets would only penetrate the wood a little
way, but no men would be hurt. And we felled
trees also to strengthen the structure. When we
had done we went inside—we and the best of our
slaves. While we were inside the men dragged the
machine forwards, for it went on wheels. We had
made loopholes in it also. The enemy came out and
endeavoured to get at us, but could not. So at
last we came down into the moat. Then tree-trunks
were brought to build the *boma* still higher. The
structure stood firm, and we worked till late in the
night. When we were higher than their *boma*, no
one could leave their *boma* any more. And inside
the houses were built of grass. We set them alight
during the night, and the people fled out of the
town, and many were killed and some taken
prisoners, and we set up another Sultan.'

Tippoo Tib's delight at this victory was damped
by the news that his old father had died at Tabora.
At the same time, however, came from there the
cheering intelligence that the powder presented
by Seyyid Burghash had arrived meanwhile, and

10

had already been sent on by Msabbah bin Niem, the
newly-appointed Vali of the Tanganyika district.
Thus Tippoo Tib found himself in a position to
take with him all the ivory left behind on the lake
within a measurable space of time.

At Ujiji he parted company with his old travelling companion, Muhammed bin Said. The latter
felt a longing to return to the flesh-pots of Manyema, and our hero was not sorry to hand over
to him his affairs in that country. He sent to all his
subordinates letters instructing them for the future to
acknowledge Bwana Nzige as their master, and give
up all the ivory to him. Yet he made the stipulation that his friend before departing should await the
arrival of the ammunition expected from Tabora.

When he himself was about to quit Ujiji,
Rumalisa earnestly begged him to take him with
him. In spite of his many raids in Uvinza, he had
' gathered no moss '; on the contrary, he had run
through the whole of a fortune entrusted to him by
his kinsman Juma bin Abdallah. The latter, a
friend of our traveller, had already several times
requested him by letter to send him back either his
property or Rumalisa's person.

Out of consideration for his cheated friend on the
one hand, and on the other out of pity for Rumalisa's
helplessness, Tippoo Tib allowed himself to be persuaded to take him with him to the coast at his
expense.

Many other Arabs had joined the caravan, which
marched unmolested through the now subject Uvinza.
Things did not go so well when they reached the
neighbourhood of Usoki, where the old dread of

Mirambo awoke in the Arabs once more.   For years
it had become a recognised thing that caravans no
longer took the ordinary route through inhabited
localities, but made their way through the desert
by secret tracks, known only to the initiated.   A
special reputation as guide was enjoyed by a Mnwa-
mwezi named Katutuvira.   He knew every water-
hole in the wilderness, and earned good money by
guiding trading parties that were seeking to avoid
Mirambo.

But although our travellers had secured the
much-sought-for pathfinder, they ran straight
into Mirambo's arms.   Some careless carriers had
strayed, as usual, from the watering-place, which
was reached at noon.   In their endeavours to find
honey in the bush, they ventured somewhat further
from the camp than was advisable, and suddenly
found themselves in face of the advance-guard of
a force of the dreaded chief.   Four were taken
prisoners, and the rest fled back to the camp with the
terrible news ' Mirambo is coming.'   All preparations
for defence were speedily made, but scarcely had
they begun to drag thorn-bushes to the spot for
a zareba, when the captives returned in good case
and reported that they had parted on the best of
terms from Mirambo's warriors.   When these learned
that they belonged to Tippoo Tib, they at once
treated them as friends, and told them their master
had strictly forbidden them to harm him or his men.
Soon after envoys came from Mirambo and exchanged
greetings and presents with the Arabs.   Next morning Tippoo Tib saw the whole train pass ; it was an
imposing force on its return from a successful raid.

Without further adventure the traveller reached Tabora, where unhappily he did not find his aged father living. His stepmother, Nyaso, however, received him with all honour, and he, too, showed her all the respect due to the wife of his deceased sire. Not long before his death the latter had laid her tenderly on Tippoo Tib's breast with the touching words : ' Man knows not the hour of his death. If I die, look to thy mother, Nyaso, daughter of Fundi Kira, and that with both eyes, if thou wishest that I should be satisfied with thee.' And he had replied : ' If God will, she shall be even better off than in thy lifetime.'

Muhammed bin Masud had meanwhile made himself useful by conveying all the ivory stored at Tabora to the coast. So there remained to be transported only what had just been brought from Tanganyika. As it was just the season for tilling the fields, and carriers were not to be had, Tippoo Tib determined for the present to proceed without loads and leave the care of the ivory to his brother.

His plans, however, were crossed by a fresh invitation from Mirambo. Either he was to come himself or send his son Sef on a visit. Tippoo Tib determined on the latter, but encountered resistance from the Arabs at Tabora. They did not believe in the peaceful intentions of their old enemy, and prophesied that Sef would certainly be murdered. Tippo Tib answered them in his superior way : ' Then it does not matter.'

He had just then a large caravan ready to proceed to Ujiji. He now caused it to take the road to Urambo, and young Sef, richly provided with

presents for the chief, joined it. His reception at
Mirambo's town was, if we may believe the autobiography, a most brilliant one.

The Arabs were furious that Tippoo Tib was so
friendly towards their enemy. They were animated
by a blind hatred against Mirambo, who had
done them many an evil turn, and although
peaceful intercourse would have been to their
interest, they would not hear of a compromise with
the insolent unbeliever. While they, like their
fathers and brothers, had for years risked life and
property in their feud with him, Tippoo Tib had
been attending to his selfish interests in Manyema.
He knew nothing of the righteous hatred which the
loss of kinsmen who had fallen in war, the plundering of rich convoys, and the murder of numberless
slaves, had nourished in their hearts. Just because
it suited him they were to forego their most precious
prize—revenge! Well, they were much obliged for
the offer of a peace which they did not want, and
they recoiled from no means of ruining the prospects
of conciliation.

After having tried in vain to hold Sef and his
people back from the trip by gloomy prognostica-
tions, they devised a frightful snare to entice him
and his caravan to destruction.

They sent ten Wanyamwezi disguised as men of
the coast to Mirambo, informing him that Seyyid
Burghash had sent a great army from the coast to
the support of the Arabs, and would shortly attack
him with superior numbers; they, the ten men,
had escaped on the road to give him timely warning.
Their whole bearing and dress were calculated

to obtain credence. 'They looked like people who had come from a journey.'

The Arabs had hoped that Mirambo, as soon as he received this news, would at once seize young Sef, and if he did not kill him, at least keep him so long as a hostage that a subsequent reconciliation would be impossible. But he did not allow himself to be taken in so easily. He told Tippoo Tib's son what had been secretly alleged, but added that he did not believe the story. Far from doing his guests any harm, all he thought of was that no unpleasantness should result to them from the stories told. He begged Sef to get the other Arabs to depart with their caravans, for as soon as the story became further known, their Wanyamwezi would get frightened and return to Tabora; then they would have no more carriers and would suffer great losses.

The Arabs acted on the suggestion, and Sef too, some days later, returned with valuable presents to his native town.

In the days when Sef paid Mirambo this memorable visit, Wissmann, then on his way from the West Coast, was also a guest of the dreaded chief. He depicts* Mirambo as a man of tall and sinewy build, placid, attractive features, and gentle speech. His exterior and bearing gave no hint that he was the hero before whom for ten years past hundreds of Arabs and thousands of natives had trembled. Mirambo very hospitably offered the German traveller entertainment, and showed him with pride his exten-

* Wissmann, 'Unter deutscher Flagge quer durch Africa,' chap. xiii. (Berlin, 1899).

sive arsenal, in which many guns, great quantities of
powder, and innumerable spears, bows, and arrows
were stored. We also learn from Wissmann the
date when Sef made his entry—August 31, 1882.
The European traveller describes Tippoo Tib's son
as a young man of twenty with a chivalrous bearing.
His handsome exterior was spoiled by a furtive glance,
and he certainly afterwards afforded Wissmann
proofs of a spiteful disposition. Tippoo Tib clung
with especial affection to this his eldest son, and
never quite got over his early death, of which we
shall hear later.

Of the exact circumstances under which Tippoo
Tib's mission was sent Wissmann gives a somewhat different account. He says the desire to
make peace originated with our hero, who, as the
Uvinza route was made precarious in consequence
of Mirambo's constant raids, desired to secure a road
through his territory for his caravans of costly
goods. He also says that Mirambo posed as a bene-
factor towards Sef, and received the son of the
famous traveller politely, it is true, but treated him
throughout as a suppliant.

It is hardly doing an injustice to the future
Imperial Commissioner if one ventures to doubt
whether at that time, when he came from the West as
a perfect stranger, he had a just appreciation of the
state of affairs. There is much in favour of Tippoo
Tib's statement that Mirambo desired peace. He
had, as Wissmann himself acknowledges, great
stores of ivory, which he could not turn to account
against the will of the Arabs. Even if he succeeded
by means of his military superiority in carrying his

caravans through the forbidden region of the Tabora
people, it was still necessary to convey the ivory
to the purchaser on the coast. Now, the natural
ally of the Tabora Arabs was their Sultan at
Zanzibar. He could at any time lay an embargo on
the treasures that had safely reached the sea as a
war indemnity for his subjects, and then all the
trouble of sending the convoys so far would be
wasted.

Wissmann himself mentions later on that
Mirambo was thoroughly desirous of making peace
with Seyyid Burghash. And to whom could he
have applied rather than Tippoo Tib, with whom
he was connected by family traditions, who cherished
no personal grudge against him, as he had been
absent during the principal conflicts, and who,
having regard to the importance of his caravans,
could only profit from peaceful relations ? Perhaps
Wissmann attached too much significance to the
official dignity with which the powerful Sultan met
the young Arab. In any case, it was to the interest
of both to make peace, and it was only natural that
both did their best finally to attain it.

Wissmann also speaks of the legend regarding
the army supposed to have been sent by Seyyid
Burghash, though in a somewhat altered form.

He learned from Sef that his father meant to
proceed very shortly to Zanzibar. As he had but
a few men with him, and on the way to Tanganyika
had learned to his cost to what risks an insufficiently
protected caravan was exposed, he determined to
join the Arab chief on his further march to the
coast.

On September 5 he reached Tabora, and drew up
at the Catholic mission-house, a large *tembe* with a
roomy veranda. The year before the White Fathers
of the Algerian Mission had made their abode here,
and had already left their mark on the country
round.

Wissmann here had the opportunity of observing
that, in contradistinction to the Evangelical missions,
which chiefly devoted themselves to doctrinal
efforts, the Catholics attached more importance to
practical training in civilization. With but narrow
means at their disposal, they had installed themselves admirably. Gardening, agriculture, and
cattle-breeding flourished under their guidance.
He was bidden welcome with the cheering hospitality usual in the wilds.

Two days later he paid Tippoo Tib—to whom he
handed a letter of recommendation from his son—
a visit in his town of Ituru. He describes him
graphically as ' a man of about forty-five and quite
black in complexion, although his father was a pure
Arab. Somewhat stout, he is yet very quick in his
movements, graceful and polite, decided in his
gestures, yet has often, like his son, a touch of
watchfulness and furtiveness, and seems to be fond
of mocking.'

This fondness for mockery, which at once struck
Wissmann during his short visit, is indeed a
characteristic of our hero which he retained till
his old age. The statement that his father was a
pure Arab is erroneous, as may be remembered
from the second chapter.

Wissmann then told him about his journey,

during which he had often come in contact with
Tippoo Tib's people, and everywhere been well
treated by them. Then he expressed the wish that
the sheikh would take him with him to the coast,
and advance him the articles necessary for the
journey. Tippoo Tib agreed to this, and September 27 was fixed as the day for setting out together.

Well armed as the caravan was, yet it could
not evade the numerous attempts at extortion on
the part of the natives at Ugogo. There was a
great drought in the country, and the few water-
holes were jealously watched, the use of them
not being conceded until after the payment of a
considerable *hongo*. Unluckily also, the small-pox
broke out in the convoy, claiming several victims
daily, and forcing its leader to be exceptionally
compliant.

Both travellers speak of these mishaps, Tippoo
Tib using the opportunity to present himself again
as an angel of unselfishness. He says that the
Wagogo only meant their demands for *hongo* for
the Christian, but that, in order to spare Wissmann unpleasantness, he paid it all, without parley,
out of his own pocket.

After a last wretched march through the cheer-
less Marenga Mkali, Mpapwa was reached at the
end of October. Wissmann, who had gone on
ahead with a small body, got there first, unmolested.
Tippoo Tib's caravan was surprised on the way by
robbers, and suffered considerable losses in goods
and lives. At Mpapwa their ways parted. Wissmann took the north road by Mamboge, and reached
the coast near Saadani on November 15. He had

thus, as he proudly boasts at the end of his book of travels, brought to a glorious conclusion the first crossing of the continent under the German flag. He was, moreover, the first man to make, from west to east, the journey already accomplished by Cameron and Stanley. And if anything goes to justify a biography of Tippoo Tib it may well be the fact that he was the faithful guide, and had no small share in the success of these three pioneers in the crossing of Africa.

CHAPTER XI

'Mene, mene, tekel, upharsin.'—DAN. v. 25.

TIPPOO TIB marched through Usagara to Bagamoyo, where he deposited his loads with the then agent of Taria Topan, the Indian Jan Muhammed Hansraj, who afterwards attained to wealth and high position in Zanzibar. That same day he started in a dhow for Zanzibar, and reached his home on the 9th of Mohurram, 1300 (November 22, 1882). Although he did not land till nearly ten in the evening, he at once sought out his creditor, who knew already from Rumalisa, who had been sent on before, that Tippoo Tib would follow directly. The Indian surprised him by the question whether he felt inclined to become Vali of Tabora, as the former Viceroy, Abdullah bin Nasib, had been recalled. Our traveller replied with a smile that he was King of a far larger country than the whole of Tabora, and was in a position to keep several Valis on his own account. Taria answered that Seyyid certainly entertained the idea of offering him the post at Tabora, and would feel greatly humiliated in his pride as Sultan if Tippoo met the offer with a curt refusal; he must at least make a show of considering the proposal.

156

Next morning he again called on Taria, and found there a Belgian, who proposed to him to undertake a journey with him to Manyema. He, the Belgian, would supply guns and ammunition, while Tippoo Tib was to find the necessary carriers. The proceeds of the journey were to be divided equally. Tippoo Tib replied that he was a subject of the Sultan of Zanzibar, to whom, as a matter of course, his other territories were subject ; if the latter gave his consent he would think the matter over. The Belgian represented to him, on the contrary, that he was sole ruler in Manyemaland, and the Sultan had no authority over him. Tippoo Tib, however, persisted that he could undertake nothing without the Sultan's sanction.

That same morning he paid his visit to Seyyid Burghash, whose acquaintance he had not yet made. He had much to tell him about his successes in West Africa, and finally reported also the proposal of the Belgian. Burghash thereupon answered that he had really had it in his mind to make him Vali of Tabora, but from what he heard of his influence in Manyemaland and the plans of the European, he considered it more advisable that Tippoo Tib should return speedily to his dominions, so as not to leave them a prey to the desires of the Western traveller. Tippoo Tib begged for a respite, at least until the whole of his ivory had arrived from Tabora, but the Sultan pressed for a speedy departure.

However, our hero soon found excuses enough, with the usual Arab faculty of procrastination, to stay a considerable time at Zanzibar.

In the first place, Wissmann arrived, some

days later, and had to be reckoned with. Tippoo
Tib says he only charged him for the goods
advanced at cost price, and said nothing about the
tolls paid for him at Ugogo.

Our traveller had also to hold consultations with
the British Consul-General, his old · acquaintance
Sir John Kirk. He was particularly interested in
the state of affairs at Ugogo, whose inhabitants
had already given rise to many complaints by the
systematic extortions they practised on passing
caravans. He proposed to Tippoo Tib to devise
means, in concert with Seyyid Burghash, to bring
the country wholly under his control. If the Sultan
had taken this hint—if, as easily might have been
done at that time, he had secured the roads to Ugogo
by adequate military posts, and thrown large bodies
of troops into the country—he would have been just
in time to avert the loss of his great possessions in
Africa. When, two years later, the chiefs of the
districts lying between Ugogo and the coast submitted to the German Protectorate, the Sultan's
protest passed unnoticed, because he could not
prove that he had ever exercised substantive rights
of sovereignty in those districts.

But Seyyid Burghash always had much less
inclination for the extension of his political influence
than for commercial undertakings. This observation was made at this very time by Wissmann when,
on reaching Zanzibar, he duly paid his visit to the
Sultan. Quite uneducated, as all the Oman Arabs
still are, he had no conception of the vast tracts
which his subjects had explored and subjugated in
his name ; and when Wissmann told him of the

many countries through which he himself had passed, the only question that interested him was whether there was much gold and silver there. When he replied in the negative and could not even give satisfactory information as to the presence of coal, the interest of the Sultan was at an end. No other points of view existed for him.

Now his thoughts were only concentrated on the commercial opening-up of the districts extolled by Tippoo Tib as rich in ivory and slaves, and he endeavoured, disregarding the political necessity of keeping the route to them open under all circumstances, first and foremost to secure a monopoly of trade for his subjects in the new regions.

In accordance with the Sultan's plenary powers at that time, he promulgated a decree, mainly directed against the Belgian, that no one should enlist carriers until Hamed bin Muhammed was sufficiently supplied. Taria was once more made to open an unlimited credit for him, and this time, after the first speculation had turned out so well, and Tippoo Tib been so successful, probably was not unwilling to do so. Personally the Sultan heaped many tokens of his favour on the famous traveller. He presented him with 2,000 rupees in cash, besides rich stuffs and other things that delight the heart of the Oriental—fragrant perfumes, richly-adorned weapons, a gold watch, and a diamond ring.

On this fresh journey Tippoo Tib took with him his newly-acquired friend Rumalisa. He had, indeed, intended to trade on his own account, but could not (as the autobiographer spitefully insists, in

view of the enmity that afterwards arose between
them) get anyone to lend him a farthing. Rumalisa's brother Nasor was also taken as a companion.

At Tabora our hero found letters from his cousin
Bwana Nzige. He complained that the people in
Manyema had become refractory, and that he felt
powerless against them. If Tippoo Tib did not
come very quickly, he would expose himself to
heavy losses, for much ivory lay ready for him.

Tippoo Tib at once determined to march on, but
could get no carriers at Tabora, as it was just harvest
time. In his need he applied to Mirambo, who at
once, like a true friend, sent him 200 men. Tippoo
Tib armed them and set off. His merchandise, to
the value of 80,000 dollars, he left to the care of
Rumalisa, who was to collect more carriers and then
to follow.

As our hero, being sure of Mirambo's friendship,
meant to take the shorter road through his country,
the Arabs again endeavoured to sow discord between
them. They made out to Tippoo Tib that he would
certainly be attacked by Mirambo, and tried to
persuade the latter that he was coming to make war
on him. But once more their slanders failed.
Tippoo Tib was received with all honour, and
Mirambo again requested him to intercede that
he might secure final peace with Seyyid Burghash.
He reported that he had on a previous occasion sent
the Sultan a great supply of ivory, but the present
had been declined ; now he meant again to send
him forty tusks, and Tippoo Tib must try to convince him of the sincerity of his peaceful intentions.

Tippoo Tib parted from his host on the best

of terms, and on the 29th Rajeb, 1300 (beginning
of June, 1883), reached the Arab settlement of
Kwa Kassongo.   Next day he visited his friends at
Nyangwe.

After a short stay he continued his march to
Sultan Lusuna, with whose help he got together a
large force.   With the energy characteristic of him,
he soon restored order throughout his territories.
While he was engaged in setting up new Valis,
a letter reached him from old Juma Mericano, who
was in great distress in a country north-west of the
Lomami, the Sultan of which, Kassongo Karambo,
had falsely persuaded him that he could do excellent business in ivory there.   When he got there it
turned out that the ruler had simply intended to
cheat the stranger out of his merchandise.   He
forbade his subjects to sell ivory direct to the Arab;
Juma had to buy it all from the Sultan himself at
high prices, and did not receive permission to leave
the country till he had found a purchaser for all
his goods.

But matters were brought to a crisis by the
fact that the Sultan had been audacious enough to
claim as his property several tusks of Tippoo Tib's
that had been handed over to Juma.   This gave our
friend the desired excuse for extending his authority
to this country.

On the way there he did some advantageous
strokes of business at Ukosi.   How he went about
the work he does not say in his biography, only
he remarks, significantly enough, that as soon as he
approached all the Shensis ran away and gave him
the new sobriquet of Mkangwansara.   The meaning

11

of this title is said to have been ' He is afraid of
nothing, or only fears that he and his men should
not find enough provisions.'

The country was rich in copper. In six days he
' acquired ' 700 *frasilas*. He then marched in
a northerly direction through thickly populated
localities, and at length reached the capital of
Kassongo, Karombo. There he found some 3,000
adults, one and all drunk. He only came across one
Muhammedan, a young man from the coast named
Musa. His friend Juma was among the drunken,
for which reason our traveller does not reckon him
as a co-religionist. Painfully the old sinner dragged
himself to the *barasa* of his house to welcome his
deliverer. But the greeting came to an abrupt conclusion by Juma at once falling into a leaden sleep.

When his renegade friend had become sober next
morning, Tippoo Tib held a most categorical palaver
with the Sultan, which ended in his not only handing over all the goods he had stolen, but giving him
ten tusks of ivory in addition as compensation.

Tippoo Tib's task was thus completed. Juma
Mericano, however, who had still various items of
business on hand, could not get away so quickly.
He begged his friend to go on alone for the present,
but first to exert all his influence that no hindrances
might be placed in the way of his departure
later on.

When this had also been satisfactorily arranged,
Tippoo Tib got under way. During his return
march he had opportunities for remarkable studies
in civilization. In almost every place he came
across people with ears and noses cut off. These

mutilations had been inflicted on them by Rungu
Kabare, a Sultan who had once held sway over
the whole of Urua. In order to give visible expression to his power he had, according to justice
or caprice, treated his subjects in this way. He
had held absolute sway far away to the east, and
would, Tippoo Tib thinks, have made even Ujiji
and Tabora unsafe, but that the great Lake Tanganyika checked his advance.

In his expeditions he used his mutilated subjects
as bogies. He placed them in the foremost ranks,
and as soon as the enemy caught sight of the earless
and noseless *promachi*, they were so stricken with
panic that they promptly took to flight.

After Rungu Kabare's death, his son Kassongo
Rushie succeeded him ; but he was unable to maintain the power of his father. Many disputes arose
between the various descendants, which soon split
up the once powerful kingdom.

Tippoo Tib passed through the province of
Ngongo, who remained, as before, a loyal and freely-
paying subject of his master, back to Nyangwe. He
only stayed there a month, and then marched on
down-stream to the so-called Stanley Falls, where, as
their most easterly *point d'appui*, the International
Congo Company had meanwhile established a
fortified station.

It will not be out of place to give here a short
sketch of the events which led to the founding of
the independent Congo State.

In September, 1876, the King of the Belgians
summoned an 'International Conference to consider
the means for the systematic exploration of Africa,'

at Brussels. To this meeting the presidents of all
the larger geographical societies were invited, and
representatives of almost all the European States
attended it. The King, who opened the Conference
in person at his palace, proposed to form an International Society for the Exploration and Civilization
of Central Africa. The proposal was received with
enthusiasm, and in connection with the Association
Internationale Africaine thus created, numerous
national committees were formed in the States
concerned, with the object of concentrating the
colonial aspirations of the various countries, and
advancing them in accordance with the principles
adopted by the International Union. The ideals
aimed at were scientific exploration on a harmonious
plan, the opening of ways of communication by
which trade and civilization might penetrate into
the interior, and the devising of means for the
suppression of slavery. For the carrying out of
these objects stations were as far as possible to
be founded, which were to make scientific observation of the tracts within their reach, and afford
hospitality to passing travellers.

The widespread interest which the Dark Continent had for some time excited developed into
general enthusiasm when, in August, 1877, Stanley
returned from his eventful crossing of Africa,
and related marvellous stories of the alleged
wealth of the tracts he had passed through. After
his unexampled success he seemed the right man
for the objects of the Association Internationale
Africaine.

After his attempt to exploit commercially the

countries he had discovered with the help of English capital had been wrecked by the backwardness of the capitalists, who, not satisfied with brilliant descriptions, demanded material guarantees, Stanley in 1878 began negotiations in Brussels. These led to the foundation, under the presidency of King Leopold, of a Comité d'Études du Haut Congo, under the auspices of which Stanley took charge of a splendidly equipped expedition. The outfit, which included a steamboat of 25 tons, four launches, and a large number of boats and lighters, was despatched by special steamer to the mouth of the Congo, while Stanley himself proceeded to Zanzibar to recruit the necessary men there.

On August 21, 1879, the expedition started up the Congo; but, as is often the case, the successful explorer did not prove a skilful organizer. True, a number of stations were established in the region of the lower Congo, but all these undertakings swallowed up great sums of money, and not the slightest trace was to be found on the spot of the stores of wealth which the country was said to possess. Moreover, the ideal aims of the Association Internationale, under whose banner the enterprise had come into existence, were not furthered in any visible way.

People at Brussels were already beginning to get very impatient when Stanley succeeded once more, by a personal sojourn in Belgium, in creating a feeling in favour of his mission, and though all his very extensive demands were not acceded to, yet very ample means were once more placed at his disposal.

At the end of 1882 he returned to the Congo. Ideal aspirations had ceased to produce any effect, and commercial enterprises for the present promised no result ; so, in order to have something to show the wondering world, the preponderance was transferred to political acquisitions. Rights of sovereignty were acquired from the various chiefs, and the newly-created stations sprang like mushrooms from the soil. Forty of them were to be counted as far as the Stanley Falls. Their establishment had, it is true, cost £600,000, and after a short time all but a few of them were given up.

In the middle of 1884 Stanley again returned to Europe, and was replaced in the conduct of the Belgian enterprises by the English Colonel Sir Francis de Winton.

Soon afterwards the districts acquired in Central Africa received their political status. They were formed into the Congo Free State (État Indépendant du Congo). King Leopold II., with the assent of the Belgian Chambers, became the head of a new political entity, which was solemnly proclaimed at Bawana on July 13, 1885.

Shortly before the so-called Congo Conference had sat at Berlin, and between November 15, 1884, and February 26, 1885, had discussed general ordinances regulating the freedom of trade in the Congo basin and the surrounding districts, the limitation of the slave trade, the neutrality of the free trade sphere, navigation on the Congo and Niger, as also the principles of future acquisitions of territory in Africa.

The furthest station established by the Belgians

was, as we have said, Stanley Falls, which Tippoo
Tib now visited. From this point he sent out
twenty large caravans to travel through the country,
which was already further opened up. Most of
these met with success, but the largest, under the
Arab Salum bin Muhammed, was almost entirely
wiped out. It went up the Aruwimi River, and
there, while making itself at home in a deserted
township, was surprised by the inhabitants returning by night, and was slaughtered and devoured
almost to a man. This disastrous adventure was,
as we shall see, to have a momentous sequel in the
future history of our hero.

While Tippoo Tib remained in these districts,
which were daily falling more and more completely under Belgian rule, he received from Seyyid
Burghash letters urging him to use every means in
his power to keep the country under his influence.
Tippoo Tib replied that he himself was powerless
without weapons and ammunition; if the Sultan
wished him to do his best for him, he must first
supply him with the necessary material. Thereupon Burghash called him back to talk over the
situation in Manyemaland with him in person.

CHAPTER XII

'Prophets right and prophets left,
The worldling in the middle.'
GOETHE : *Dinner at Coblenz.*

TIPPOO TIB quickly settled his outstanding affairs,
and started for Tanganyika with a fresh store of
ivory—900 *frasilas*, as he says. On the way
messengers reached him from Rumalisa with no
very edifying news. There was war at Uvinza, and
Tippoo Tib's merchandise, which represented a
considerable capital, was in danger of being wholly
lost if he could not at once place a large body of
troops at Rumalisa's disposal. Acting on this
advice, our hero sent 500 warriors, armed with
guns, on ahead in all haste, and followed himself
by forced marches. At Ujiji he found Rumalisa,
to whom he gave further instructions for the conflict. Then he marched away to Tabora, reaching
the town of his fathers in September, 1886.

Here, too, in spite of the short time he had spent
beyond Tanganyika, he found many things changed,
to the disadvantage of his compatriots. If the
Belgians on the west had seriously curtailed the
Arab influence, on the east the Germans were

threatening more and more to force backwards the Oriental sphere of power.

On April 3, 1884, the Society for German Colonization had been founded at Berlin, and at the end of the same year Dr. Peters had, under its orders, started on his famous flag-hoisting journey, which ended in the peaceful subjugation of the territories of Useguha, Nguru, Usegara, and Ukami. On February 27, 1885, the Emperor, William I., sanctioned the acquisition of the new districts by the issue of a charter. On April 25 Sultan Burghash was officially informed of the fact, and at once raised a protest at Berlin by telegraph. He insisted that the chiefs had had no right to alienate the districts acquired by Germany, for these—so ended the very sharply worded protest—belonged to him ' since the days of his fathers.'

The claims of the Sultan were, naturally, not acknowledged by the German Foreign Office. He had certainly exercised no effective rights of sovereignty over the ceded territories. It is sufficiently demonstrated by what has gone before that the Arabs who journeyed into the interior were habitually regarded by the natives as enemies. Almost everywhere our hero had to force a passage or purchase it by heavy payments, regulated by the caprice of the various chiefs. If the natives dealt so with the subjects of the Sultan of Zanzibar, it was quite plain that they did not fear his power, still less acknowledge his sovereignty.

That the Sultan had small military posts here and there can scarcely be taken into account. They were like oases in the desert, and their influ-

ence did not extend beyond the range of their guns.
But even the few places where there were large
colonies of Arabs, with Valis appointed by the
Sultan, cannot be regarded as belonging to Zanzibar. As the conflicts round Tabora teach us, such
Valis had no authority over the neighbouring
natives; it only extended to the Arabs and people
of the coast who lived near them. They were, in
modern phraseology, Consuls of the Sultan, invested
with jurisdiction to a certain extent, but with this
drawback—that their *exequatur* was only respected
by the local rulers as long as it brought them
advantage.

In order to break down the resistance of the
Sultan to the German acquisitions, a strong squadron
was sent in June to Zanzibar, and anchored
menacingly before his palace. On August 14
Seyyid Burghash recognised the cession of the
territories, and was clearly glad, in face of this
display of force by the German Empire, that his
whole country was not annexed. As a pendant to
these proceedings, negotiations were entered on
with England concerning the further development
of West African affairs. These resulted, on November 1, 1886, in the London Convention, which
formed the first international basis for German
colonial aspirations. The Sultan was acknowledged
as Suzerain over the islands of Zanzibar, Pemba
Lamu, and Mafia, and a belt on the coast ten
miles broad, from the Rovuma to Kipini. Germany acceded to an agreement concluded between
England and France in 1882, by which the inde-
pendence of the Sultan was guaranteed. In order

to make accessible by sea the new acquisitions of the colonizing association—which had meanwhile been transformed into the German East African Company—England promised its good offices to induce the Sultan to lease to it the customs harbours of Dar-es-salaam and Pangani.   The joint use of the former had already been conceded to the Company in September, 1885.   In addition to this, Germany and England agreed to delimit shortly their respective spheres of influence in the treaty districts.   As a supplement to this treaty, Burghash let himself be persuaded in 1887 to farm the whole of the Customs on the coast to the German Company.   A formal treaty regulating the details was signed in April, 1888, by his successor and brother, Khalife.

The economic opening up of the East Coast territories went hand-in-hand with their political conquest.   As long ago as the beginning of the nineteenth century American whale-fishers had come in contact with Zanzibar, and since 1830 the American firm of John Bertram had been firmly established there.   It sent sailing vessels from time to time to the Indian Ocean, and exchanged Western clothing materials for coffee in Arabia, and for ivory, rubber, and cloves in the East African capital. Soon afterwards the Hamburg firm of O'Swald also set up at Zanzibar.   Till then the West Coast had been its sphere of action, but in 1846 it sent a ship to the East Coast to obtain the cowrie-shells, which were current there as money.   The favourable conditions of trade found to prevail there encouraged the firm to establish a permanent settle-

ment. Near the Custom-house it acquired a piece
of land, on which it erected a house, which still
counts among the finest and most convenient buildings in the town. In 1859 the Hanse Towns established at Zanzibar a Consulate, the management of
which was entrusted to the firm. After the consular
representation was taken over, first by the North
German Confederation and later by the German
Empire, the post was held by the head of the firm
for the time being till 1884, when a regular German
Consulate was created.

In the sixties an employé who was leaving the
firm of O'Swald founded a rival establishment
for the Hamburg house of Hansing and Co., while
in 1874 the great ivory firm of H. A. Meyer set up a
branch at Zanzibar. While the two first-named
carried on business on the spot, the professional
activity of the latter gradually necessitated getting
into touch with the interior. Countries really rich
in ivory were even then scarcely to be found on this
side of Tanganyika. The nearest good market was
at Tabora, where, beside the tusks of the elephants
killed in the country, much of the ivory obtained in
Manyema was to be bought. Thither the firm in
July and August sent two representatives, named
Harders and Töppen, amply supplied with merchandise. They reached their destination at the end of
the year, and at once encountered the greatest
difficulties. The Arabs, as a matter of course,
viewed with distrust the foreign element which
desired to intrude into their midst. While the
permanent society of the unbelievers was distasteful to them, the competition of the strangers

was also to be dreaded. They worked with proper and reliable means, paid cash, and might, if left alone, end in attracting all the custom. Moreover, they were in a position to observe many Arab tricks, which, if reported on the coast, must create bad blood there. That the throne of their Sultan at Zanzibar no longer stood firm, and the accursed Franks, with their ships of war, had lately made a great display there, was not, of course, unknown to the Tabora people, thanks to their busy intercourse with the home country. Besides, of late so many strangers were going about the country, of whom no one knew rightly what they wanted. Formerly they had only laughed at the crazy fellows in tattered clothes who followed the courses of rivers of no importance, or climbed high mountains without getting any advantage thereby. But by degrees it seemed as if there was some tangible support behind these Westerners, and now that even the powerful Sultan of Zanzibar began to be subservient to them the matter was getting serious. So prudence was advisable. Open violence is contrary to the Oriental character as long as other means are at command. It is quite possible to keep an amiable countenance and harass one's enemies well at the same time. In East African legal affairs *dasturi* plays a great part : no Papal dogma is so infallible ; and it is a part of *dasturi*, and a leading one, to give presents everywhere. Those who are unaware of this fact must be told of it.

So the Vali of Tabora, a man of noble birth, named Zid bin Juma, of course took good care duly to instruct the poor ignorant strangers. Leave to settle in Tabora was not refused, but they must make him presents for it; the purchase of ivory was allowed them, but in return they must bestow on the representative of the Sultan under whose protection they lived such a part of their merchandise as seemed suitable.

As a matter of course, too, they must show their gratitude to the ruler of the country for the hospitality afforded them. Mkasiva had died in the meantime, and his son Sike reigned in his stead, who, being of a covetous nature, liked to work hand-in-hand with the Arabs to extort as much as possible from the strangers. Thus in six weeks goods to the value of some 7,000 marks were wheedled out of the new-comers with an affable smile, or in case of refusal with alarming threats. If the Vali wanted anything he made the needs of the Sultan his excuse, while the Sultan in turn sheltered himself behind the Vali when he was in an acquisitive humour.

As, owing to these one-sided proofs of friendship, but little business could be done for the firm, in March, 1886, Töppen started for the coast to seek the intervention of the German Consulate-General in getting the Sultan to alter the *dasturi* practised by his subjects; but he fell ill from sunstroke, and so his arrival at Zanzibar was delayed. But as previous complaints as to the oppression of the agents at Tabora had already reached him, the Sultan indited various letters of advice to the Vali and Sike. These were despatched by a new representative of the firm, Giesecke, who was sent to Tabora in the early part of 1886. On the way he received the sad news that Harders had died of fever. A French traveller, Révoil, had been with him at the time of his death, and had meant to hold out in Tabora until a fresh agent of the firm appeared, to whom he might hand over the stock, of which he had taken charge in the meantime. His health forced him, however, to leave before this. He made out in the presence of witnesses a careful inventory of the Meyers' property, which was afterwards delivered to Giesecke. The goods intended for exchange proved to be intact, but it was found that forty tusks, of a value of some 14,000 marks, had been abstracted. The Arab Muhammed bin Kasum was subsequently unmasked as the perpetrator of the theft. He had undermined the approach to the Meyers' *tembe*, and carried off the ivory through the opening. This is a favourite method of burglary in East Africa.

The Sultan's letters of advice were of very little use—in fact, Sike, emboldened by the attitude of the Arabs, continued his attempts at extortion more shamelessly than ever. Even the permission to bury the deceased Harders in Taboran soil had to be bought by Giesecke at the cost of some 300 marks.

In addition to all this chicanery, on May 27, soon after his arrival, an attempt was made on Giesecke's life. While he was sitting in his room one evening he was fired at through the window, and the large slugs with which the gun was loaded struck the wall a short distance from his head.

The firm, in consequence, determined to give up the settlement at Tabora; but while they were debating as to the most advantageous way of

conveying the existing stock to the coast a
second murderous attack on Giesecke was perpe-
trated, which cost him his life. At the time when
this happened Tippoo Tib had just reached Tabora,
and from this moment we can again follow his
memoranda at first hand.

He begins by recording how Giesecke told him
of his trouble as to the intrigues of the Arabs, the
purloining of the ivory, and the first attempt on
himself. He personally examined the place where
the slugs had entered the wall, and on measuring
found that the space between their marks and the
place where Giesecke had sat was only an inch.
Tippoo Tib urged Giesecke to make the journey to
the coast under his protection, and the offer was
gratefully accepted.

He then narrates that he met yet another
European at Tabora, who had passed through
Khartûm to Wadelai, seen Emin Pasha, and then
proceeded to Uganda. This was the Russian Dr.
Junker. This well-known traveller, born at
Moscow in 1840, had already made two expeditions
to the Southern Nile regions, in 1873 and 1876, and
since 1879 had been engaged in exploring the
sources of that river. He had, as Tippoo Tib quite
correctly states, come across the well-known Emin
Bey at Lado. Owing to the Mahdist rising, of
which we shall have to speak again later on, his
return by the northern route had been cut off. His
brother, who lived in Russia and feared for his life,
had sent out an expedition to his relief in 1884
under the German traveller Dr. Fischer. But he
had to turn back without effecting his purpose,

owing to the hostile action of King Mwanga of
Uganda. Junker, however, succeeded in forcing
his way for himself. Early in 1886 he started from
Wadelai, and in the beginning of September of that
year reached Unyanyembe. He took up his
residence at the English mission-station of Ujui, not
far from Tabora. Here he learnt that Tippoo Tib
would arrive in a few days and continue his march
to the coast without stopping. He naturally wished,
in view of the prevailing insecurity, to seize the
opportunity to continue his journey under the
protection of the powerful caravan leader.

To be sure, he had to pay dearly for this honour.
From diaries left behind by Giesecke we learn
that Junker paid Tippoo Tib for carriers supplied
by him the sum of 1,500 dollars. The usual tariff
for a carrier from Tabora to the coast was at that
time from 10 to 12 dollars, or at most 18 dollars,
a total in round numbers of 700 dollars. The
excess of 800 dollars was agreed on as a sort of life
insurance, payable on the safe delivery of Junker at
Zanzibar.

Tippoo Tib did not wish to stay longer than
necessary at Tabora, and so it was agreed to make
ready for departure with all speed, and start at the
end of September. In the interval the travellers
pitched their camp in Ituru, the quarter where their
protectors lived. There, in the night of the 27th,
the fatal attempt on the unfortunate Giesecke was
made. As Junker sat reading in his tent towards
eleven in the evening he was suddenly startled by
shots close at hand. At the same moment he heard
pitiful calls for help from Giesecke's tent, only

12

twenty paces away. Hastening thither at once, he found the young merchant mortally wounded. He remained all night with him, while Tippoo Tib, who had speedily come to the scene at the news of the disaster, sent messengers to the Catholic mission-station at Kiparapara to beg for further assistance. Then the Arab chief, wounded to the quick by this treacherous attack in his own camp, proceeded straight to Tabora to call the Vali Zib bin Juma to account for the breach of the peace. As to what followed we had best listen to his own descriptions.

He said to the Vali Zid : ' " You have, without any cause, wrought my destruction. It is not the European you have injured, but me." But Zid bin Juma said : " No one but Muhammed bin Kasum can have shot him. Just now in the night I heard shots. They must have come back then." Next morning Zid sent messengers out to call all the Arabs together and likewise informed the Sultan. Thereupon the same morning came messengers from Sike, who sent his servant Sungura and a message that he knew nothing about it. Yet he was in the same boat with Muhammed bin Kasum. Many Arabs also came, and Muhammed bin Kasum among them. Suddenly an Englishman also appeared who was at Urambo.

' A great examination was set on foot and the Arabs said : " We know nothing of the matter." Then up jumped Sleman bin Zahir el Gabiri, and said in the presence of Muhammed : " No one can have shot the European but Muhammed bin Kasum. He is a great robber !" Then Muhammed grew

alarmed and said : " I stole the ivory—that is true,
but I did not fire at the European. Should I kill a
man who travels with Hamed bin Muhammed ?   I
would never do such a thing."   Sleman said : " It
was you and no one else. If you bid us, Hamed bin
Muhammed, we will put him in chains and give him
to you, that you may take him to the coast."   I
said to them : " Do you people of Tabora yourselves
take him prisoner."

' Thereupon the Englishman who came from
Urambo said to me : " Let us go and see to Mr.
Giesecke."   So we went and came to Ituru, where
we found Dr. Junker.   He said to us : " The missionaries have taken Giesecke with them."   We lay
down to sleep, and next morning I went with Junker
and the Englishman to the missionaries, where we
found Giesecke.   He was sick and called me and
said : " I am sick—God knows it.   The ivory that I
have has brought me to ruin ; if you leave me in
the lurch it will all be lost.   I beg of you, take it
and give it to my friends on the coast.   Say what
you want for doing so."   I answered him : " I want
nothing for it, but tell these Europeans—the French-
men, the Englishman, and Junker—to count the
tusks, then I will take them with me."   Then he
said to me : " Leave me eight men here to look
after me."   Then I went back with the Europeans
to Ituru, where they counted the ivory.   When we
had finished the counting the missionaries went
home, and the Englishman asked me for guides to
Tabora.   Two days later we set out and reached
the coast near Bagamoyo.'

Poor Giesecke received the tenderest care among

the White Fathers, but nevertheless succumbed to
his wounds on October 3. His murderer, Muhammed
bin Kasam, thanks to the disturbed state of affairs,
long evaded the arm of justice, but at last ventured
to visit the coast, and was condemned to death
by a court-martial on June 16, 1890. On the 25th
of the same month he was hanged.

The rest of the ivory belonging to the firm of
H. A. Meyer was conscientiously delivered by
Tippoo Tib at Zanzibar. Their other claims for
compensation, which amounted to 80,000 marks in
round numbers, were only partially satisfied, in spite
of repeated representations to Seyyid Burghash and
his successor, Khalifa. A *shambe* belonging to the
murderer was confiscated for their benefit and sold
for 1,900 dollars, also a quantity of ivory belonging
to his accomplice, Zid bin Juma, which produced
some 2,000 marks, was seized on the coast.

Dr. Junker reached Zanzibar under Tippoo Tib's
guidance. He proceeded to Europe and recorded
the experiences and knowledge acquired on his
long voyages in various articles which appeared in
' Petermann's Mitteilungen,' and a larger work,
' Reisen in Afrika, 1875-1886.' He died at St.
Petersburg in 1892.

When Tippoo Tib reached the coast at Bagamoyo,
he found a letter from the Sultan summoning him
to come to him at once. He immediately obeyed,
and as soon as he reached Zanzibar was received by
Seyyid Burghash. He had much to tell the Sultan
about his last journey, and the latter learned with
sorrow how from the West also the Europeans were
pressing ever closer upon the old bulwarks of the

Arabs on the mainland. The reports of so experienced a traveller convinced him that his part in
the interior of Africa would ere long be played out.
In two voyages to Europe this clear-sighted Prince
had learned from personal observation the power of
the West, and had of late been forced to realize in
his own country how weak his Oriental despotism
was compared with the armaments of Germany and
England. He had no further aspiration than to
retain at least the remainder of his kingdom—the
island of Zanzibar itself—and he closed his interview with his subject, who had travelled so far and
saw through matters with the same hopeless perspi-
cacity, with these mournful words : ' Then he said
to me : " Hamed, be not angry with me ; I want
to have no more to do with the mainland. The
Europeans want to take Zanzibar here from me :
how should I be able to keep the mainland ?   Happy
are those who did not live to see the present state
of affairs. You are a stranger here still, but you
will see how things are going here." '

And Tippoo Tib adds with resignation : ' When
I heard these words I knew that it was all up
with us.'

CHAPTER XIII

THE FIGHTING ROUND STANLEY FALLS

'Dulce et decorum est pro patriâ mori.'
HORACE.

Two months after his arrival at Zanzibar Tippoo Tib learned that soon after his departure from Stanley Falls a violent conflict had broken out between the Arabs and Europeans, ending in the flight of the latter and the destruction of the station. The autobiographer says nothing as to the details of these events, and they might quite properly be left out here, as he himself was not present ; but the way in which the hostile parties rush at each other and the long accumulated store of explosive material breaks into flame at a touch is so characteristic, the devotion even to death of the slender body of Europeans so admirable, that it may be worth while to insert here the narrative of an eye-witness, who seems qualified beyond all others to give an account of this deplorable episode.

Deane, then the head of the station, who, as the only surviving European, defended it to the last charge of powder, and only by a miracle escaped the fury of his Arab pursuers, shortly before his death gave Herbert Ward, a traveller whom we shall

meet again in the career of our hero, a description
of his sufferings, which the latter thus reproduces
in his ' Five Years with the Congo Cannibals'
(Part II., chap. xi.) :

' You know how I was ordered to Stanley Falls
last year (1885) by the Colonel (Sir Francis de
Winton, the Administrator-General of the Congo
State) to take over command and endeavour to keep
the Arabs in order and protect the natives from their
exactions, so that the authority of the State might be
established and fully recognised by them. Well,
you remember how I got wounded in the leg by
a spear-thrust when the Monungeri savages attacked
us on the first journey up to the Falls, and how
I had to return to Stanley Pool to recover from the
effects of the wound, for we found that the spear
had been poisoned. I lay ill a long while, and it
was only in January that I was able to return to the
Falls.

' You remember—for I showed you my instructions
—how I was promised a plentiful supply of ammunition and rifles and reinforcements of men when the
river steamer *Le Stanley* made its next trip up to the
Falls, which would be in August. Well, upon my
arrival I found things in a very bad condition : the
Arabs had the entire upper hand and bullied the
natives just as they pleased ; yet I could do nothing
to prevent them, for it was too far off the time of my
expected reinforcements to provoke a conflict.

' Tippoo Tib had gone back to Zanzibar, and had
left his partner, Bwana Nzige, in charge of his
people, and Nzige's son, Rashid bin Muhammed
bin Said, also had much to say in the management

of affairs during Tippoo Tib's absence. I soon saw
that these fellows did not like me or my ways at all,
and that I should not get them to conform to my
orders without a row. I had thirty-two Haussas,
under Sergeant-Major Musa Kanu, a fine, tall fellow,
and also about forty Bangala, whom I had brought
up with me in *Le Stanley*, and I set to work to
fortify the station, clear away the grass and scrub
around it in case of a surprise, and to be able to
keep an eye on the Arabs over on the mainland.

'It is necessary to observe that the State station
of Stanley Falls was built on an island in the Congo
just below the seventh cataract, while the Arabs
were mostly on the mainland, although a few lived
in a village on the same island among the natives.

'Well, the time went on, and a worse feeling sprang
up between the Arabs and me, owing to my attempts
to protect the natives from their robberies. One
day, about the middle of July (1886), a woman
entered the camp seeking protection and saying
that the Arabs had flogged her. Her story was that
she had been given to Tippoo Tib as a pledge
of friendship by her father, but that, being of
the Wachongera Meno tribe (*i.e.*, of "the filed
teeth" tribes, who are usually cannibals), Tippoo
Tib did not care for her, and had given her to
one of his most influential Arab head-men. This
Arab ill-treated her, she said, and so she had fled to
us for protection. I could not discover any traces
of ill-treatment—there were no marks on her skin—
and I told her she must return to her Arab husband,
as I had no right to interfere unless she were being
cruelly used, and I had her conducted back to the

Arab village. After a few days she came into the station again, with her back cut with lashes from a whip and her body covered with bruises, telling us that she had been terribly flogged, and that, had she not escaped, her master would have killed her. This time there was no doubt her story was true. She was a pitiable-looking object, and I determined nothing should induce me to give her up again to the cruelty and brutality of the Arabs. It was not long before Bwana Nzige, with his son Rashid and all the principal Arabs, came over to me and demanded the woman's release. I replied that I should not think of letting her be taken away again to suffer their brutal violence, and that I was sent to the country to prevent such acts, and that, as the representative of the Congo Free State, I intended to do my duty. As the woman represented a certain value to them, I was quite prepared to pay, on behalf of the Government, whatever they should demand in reason as ransom. They sullenly declined this offer and persistently demanded the release of the woman, saying that I should regret my refusal. Then I knew that the storm which had been so long brewing was going to break. However, we were well armed, my Haussas were plucky, and the fortifications I had constructed protected us well, and I considered that, with the aid of my two Krupp guns, we could keep the Arabs at a respectful distance, and in a few days—for it was the month of August—I hoped to see *Le Stanley* arrive with reinforcements and ammunition and a white officer or two, for I was alone, as you know.

' The Arabs made no direct attack upon us,

although large numbers of their Manyemas continued to assemble on the mainland. At last *Le Stanley* was signalled early one morning coming up the river, and I was indeed delighted, for I expected she would have on board the much-needed ammunition and reinforcements. But imagine my disgust when, on getting to the landing-place, I found she had not brought me a single cartridge of the promised 10,000, not a rifle, and not a man, save only Lieutenant Dubois, of the Belgian Lancers. He turned out to be a splendid fellow; but still I needed the other things, or my fight was hopeless.

'Well, when *Le Stanley* arrived the Arabs came to the conclusion that I should prove too strong for them with my supposed reinforcements, so they sent in a deputation to intimate that hostilities were at an end, and that they desired to remain in friendly relations with the white man who represented the Congo Free State. I agreed to this, and we parted seemingly good friends, and shortly afterwards I even went so far as to visit one of their villages at the upper end of the island, and there found, to my chagrin, some of the Zanzibar crew of *Le Stanley* chatting with their compatriots among the Arabs, and telling them of my disappointment, and how the steamer had brought me none of the expected aid.

'The next day *Le Stanley* left, and Dubois was busy arranging his quarters while I glanced through the piles of newspapers that my considerate friends on the Lower Congo had sent up to me. Towards evening I was told by a friendly native that the Arabs intended attacking the station the following morning, for he had overheard their

plans. We kept strict watch during the night,
but could distinguish nothing, until at dawn we
found sure enough a large body of Manyemas had
crossed from the mainland in the night and entrenched themselves on my island, about 800 yards
from the stockade. As soon as it was light we
received a practical proof of their hostility, for
they fired upon us. We kept up a lively fire upon
them with our Snyder and Martini rifles for two
days ; but they were well sheltered by their rough
earthworks, and there were no serious losses on
either side.

' Our men kept up a tremendous fusillade when-
ever the Arabs made any signs of attacking, and
on the evening of the third day Dubois sallied out
of the stockade and penetrated into the Arab lines,
capturing a Manyema drum, which they left in their
flight. It was hot work, and he got his revolver-
pouch shot off his hip. That night they remained
quiet, but in the morning fresh earth-heaps were
found thrown up nearer our entrenchments, and
the fight recommenced. Our ammunition was now
beginning to fail, and so we could not waste so
many shots, and the Arabs took advantage of this
to make two or three rushes right up to our position ; but we drove them back each time, and I
worked the Krupp guns so hard that blood came
from my ears, and I knocked the end off my little
finger by getting it jammed in the breach. My
boys — Jack (poor little Jack from Manyanga,
down there in the valley), and the two Aruwimi
youngsters—behaved splendidly, bringing ammunition to us, and making tea and carrying the cups

up to us right across the Arab line of fire. Dubois
charged out again, and drove them back, and then
darkness set in and stopped the fight for the night.
The Bangala deserted that night, taking some
native canoes and making off down the river, to
try and reach Bangala, which, you know, is a 500
miles' journey.

'In the morning the fight started again. We
could now do little but work the Krupp guns, as
the little rifle ammunition we had left was almost
entirely bad.

'We got cap-guns and old trade flint-locks out
of the store, and gave them to the Haussas to fire ;
but seven of these poor chaps were already dead, and
the rest, save Musa Kanu and three men, came to
me that evening and said they must go. It was no
use fighting when they were bound to fall into the
hands of the Arabs. I threatened to shoot them as
deserters, and they replied :

' " Very well, master, you shoot us. We would
rather you shoot us than have our throats cut by
the Arabs."

'And as soon as darkness set in they made off
to the canoes and drifted down river after the
Bangala.

'Dubois and I were now left with only four
Haussas and Samba, a native of the Aruwimi, who
had been freed by the State, and worked faithfully
with me during all my stay at the Falls ; and
despairingly we determined to destroy that night
all that we could of the stores remaining, to spike
the guns and blow up the station, and make off
into the woods, to hide until relief should come

from Bangala, where we reckoned the fugitive Bangalas would arrive by a certain date, and Coquilhat would hurry up in the steamer *Association Internationale Africaine* to our relief. We sprinkled the stores with oil, piled up the cartridges, spiked the Krupps, and gathered all the loose gunpowder together, and, having set a train to this outside the station, we two, with Musa Kanu and his three faithful Haussas and Samba, who refused to budge without us, made off under cover of the darkness to gain the north shore, and seek shelter in the woods there.

' I was the last to leave the place, and I set fire to the train of powder and made after the rest.

'The night was pitch dark, and the station was blazing brightly behind us, but somehow the powder had not exploded. We knew the Arabs must have discovered our flight by this time, so we hurried along to cross over to the mainland. We had to wade through an arm of the Congo—a rushing torrent of water, about 50 yards wide and generally at that season only waist-deep. Dubois slipped on the rocks, and was swept down into deeper water. I knew he could not swim, so I at once jumped in after him, and managed to catch hold of him before he was carried away by the swift current. We were just able to reach the steep rocky bank, and, exhausted, I told Dubois to hold on to the edge of a jutting rock, while the Haussas, having safely passed over, came to our assistance along the top of the bank. Musa Kanu undid his belt and gun-strap, tied them together, and lowered them to me; but when I turned where

Dubois had been, saying, " Catch hold here !" I could see nothing of him. There was no Dubois.

' By the light of the burning station, where the cartridges and gunpowder had now commenced to explode, illuminating vividly for a moment the surrounding scene, I searched the water for any signs of Dubois; but alas, poor fellow! he had become numbed in the water, or his heavy boots pulled him down, and he had been swept away by the current. It was the last I ever saw of him, and my grief and misery were so great at the loss of my only friend away up here, after all the pluck he had shown during the four days' fighting at the station, that I wept, while the Haussas, after pulling me up, cried too.

' We were indeed a wretched lot. My clothes had been burnt off me and torn in the fight. I had only an old blanket round me and a shirt on, but no boots; and sadly, and feeling that I didn't care if the Arabs should find me and end the wretchedness at once, I crept away into the forest.'

There he remained for thirty days, often on the verge of starvation, and hunted by the Arabs from one hiding-place to another, till at last the steamer *Association Internationale Africaine* from Bangala brought him deliverance. After all, a long life was not in store for him. When he had restored his shattered health in England, he returned to the Congo State, and met his death in an elephant hunt in the forests of the Lukolela. His station remained for the time in the hands of the Arabs, till the events occurred which we shall describe in the next chapter.

CHAPTER XIV

THE EMIN PASHA EXPEDITION

' Nihil est quod noscere malim
Quam fluvii causas per sæcula tanta latentes,
Ignotumque caput, spes sit mihi certa videndi
Niliacos fontes.'

LUCAN : *Pharsalia.*

MENTION has been made in a previous chapter of
the Egyptian general Emin Pasha. Such is the
name under which in the eighties of last century
Edmund Schnitzer, a German savant, became
known to the whole civilized world. He was born,
in 1840, at Oppeln, of Jewish parents, afterwards
became a convert to Christianity, and studied
medicine and science at Breslau. In 1865 he
became port physician at Antivari, in Albania, and
from 1873 on made lengthy journeys in Armenia,
Syria, and Arabia in the suite of a Turkish dignitary. In 1876 he entered the Egyptian service
as Emin Effendi, and was there attached to the
staff of Governor-General Gordon. With him he
travelled about Khartum and Uganda. In 1879 he
was promoted to be Bey, and appointed Governor
of the Equatorial Province. Here he found the
chance of bringing his great administrative talents

191

into play. His district, till then the scene of
devastating slave-raids, soon recovered its prosperity under his rule. He established new stations,
which made the country secure, and constructed an
extensive network of roads. By the introduction of
new cereals he forwarded agriculture, while cattle-
breeding, which had been much neglected during
years of fighting, soon attained its old importance,
thanks to the peaceful progress of the country. In
addition, Emin rendered great services to knowledge in the most various fields. As a geographer,
he explored the still little known country round
Lake Victoria. An exceptionally gifted linguist,
he diligently studied the languages of the districts
he passed through, and he benefited natural science
by rich ornithological collections.

While he was thus engaged in the peaceful work
of civilization in the heart of Africa, bloody conflicts
were taking place in the North of Egypt. The
growing influence of England and France on the
government of the country had for years been
awaking a feeling of hostility to foreigners. In
June, 1882, a revolt broke out in Alexandria, insti-
gated by the former War Minister, Arabi, in which
many Europeans fell victims. The city was in
consequence bombarded by the British Admiral
Seymour on July 11 and 12 ; but the only result
of this step was that the fury of the populace against
the foreigners was augmented. True, the English
managed, on September 13, to defeat Arabi at Tel-
el-Kebir and take him prisoner, and bring the
Khedive, who had fled on the outbreak of the
revolt, back to Cairo ; but it was only a seeming

peace which had been imposed. Already the
national Islamic movement had found a new leader
in Muhammed Ahmed, the Mahdi, who, under the
pretext of a Divine mission, incited religious
fanaticism and political discontent to take arms
against the helpless central authority. Several
brilliant victories which he gained over considerable armies commanded by English generals soon
made him master of the whole of the Sudan, which
intruded itself like a huge wedge between the seat
of the Egyptian Government and Emin's district.
After April 14, 1883, the latter found himself cut
off from all communication with North Egypt.*
Even in his own province the situation was beginning to be critical. The Mahdists, pressing further
and further forward, tried to incite his subjects to
join their movement, and in May, 1884, one of his
higher officials, Ibrahim Aga, formally repudiated
his authority. When, in addition, in 1885, a famine

---

* Since 1883 there had been in Emin's neighbourhood and
under his protection two European travellers, who had escaped
from the neighbouring countries, Dr. Junker, already mentioned, and Gaetano Casati, an Italian ex-officer, who since
1880 had been exploring for the Società d'Esploracione Com-
merciale in Bahr el Ghazal and the Mombuttu countries.
Both fugitives shared for three years the cares and perils to
which Emin was exposed in his forlorn post, and repaid the
hospitality shown them by much active support. Early in
1886 Junker, as we have seen, departed via Unyamwezi to
the coast, while Casati proceeded in May of the same year to
negotiate with King Kabarega, but was treated there more as
a prisoner than as a guest, and in the end actually condemned
to death. On the approach of Stanley he was set at liberty,
and in 1889 went on with him and Emin to the East
Coast.

broke out in the north of his territory, between
Lado and Dufilé, Emin found himself compelled to
withdraw further to the southward. He went up
the Nile to Wadelai, which he reached on July 10,
and which became for the future the seat of his
government.

Early in 1886 Emin received from Cairo the
official announcement that the whole Sudan was
abandoned. It was left to his own discretion to
remain or go. Emin for some time entertained the
idea of marching to the East Coast, but his troops
refused to follow him. Besides, the plan would
have been wrecked by the hostility of King Mwanga,
of Uganda, who, as will be remembered, had about
the same time refused a passage through his territories to Fischer, who was marching to Emin's
relief.

While Emin thus clung to his post, cut off from
all the world, a committee for his relief was forming
under the presidency of Sir William Mackinnon,
Bart. The subscriptions, to which the Egyptian
Government contributed £10,000, quickly reached
the total of £21,500. With this sum an expedition
was to be sent to try and get through to the Pasha
and release him from his dangerous position. The
American Stanley, then at the zenith of his fame,
was fixed on as the leader of the enterprise. After
carefully weighing the possible routes, four in all,
which came under consideration, he decided to
advance from the mouth of the Congo to the Albert
Nyanza, near which Emin must be located. By
this river, which has the most abundant flow of
water in Africa, one could go by steamer, with

few slight interruptions, caused by the well-known
cataracts, as far as the mouth of the Aruwimi, and
then follow that stream up to Yambuya. After that
there were about 400 miles to march, through
districts which, it is true, were totally unknown,
and probably covered with the densest forest ; but
Stanley had ere now overcome so many difficulties
that such prospects could not daunt him. King
Leopold not only gave a ready assent to the
expedition traversing the Congo State, but placed
at their disposal the Free State's entire supply of
boats for the voyage up the Congo.

But there was a serious objection to this route—
viz., the probable attitude of the Arabs. After the
conflicts described in the last chapter, it was to be
feared that they would treat any European passing
through as an enemy. But Stanley had a brilliant
idea for coping with this contingency too. He
determined on nothing less than obtaining the
co-operation in his enterprise of the leader of those
very Arabs—our hero, Tippoo Tib.

From Egypt, where he had been negotiating with
the Government, Stanley proceeded, early in 1887,
to Zanzibar. He arrived there in February, and
found everything in good order for a start. The
firm of Smith, Mackenzie and Co. had engaged
carriers for him, provided the necessary goods, and
got ready the steamer *Madura*, which was to carry
the expedition round the Cape to the Congo. His
first care at Zanzibar was to come to an understanding with Tippoo Tib. The negotiations were
carried on at the British Consulate-General. The
entry of our hero seems to have been most dramatic.

His adherents had sent him from Stanley Falls three Krupp shells, which he had had carried after him. Pointing to them, he said to Stanley that such were the presents he had to expect from Europeans. Stanley earnestly urged him to let bygones be bygones. Those conflicts had been brought about through the unfortunate misunderstandings of young people, and both sides had paid dearly for their hot-headedness. The King of the Belgians, at any rate, desired peace with the Arabs, and as a proof of it offered him, Tippoo Tib, the post of Governor in the province wrested from the Congo State by the Arab bands.

The King had, in fact, given his consent by telegraph to this proposal, but the idea originated with Stanley, and does all honour to his political sagacity. There was no simpler way of check-mating his opponents than by making their leader his friend. And Stanley saw through his man clearly enough to be certain that his offer would not be rejected. Tippoo Tib soon recovered his Oriental repose in face of the propitiatory attitude of Stanley, and received his surprising proposal with his own peculiar blink, a sign with him of quick understanding. After the conditions had been conveyed to him in detail, he gave his consent. He was engaged at a monthly salary of £30, for which he was to pledge himself to hoist the Belgian flag and restrain his fellow-tribesmen from slave-hunting and other marauding. A European official was attached to him, who was to make regular reports to the King of the Belgians, and whose duty it was, besides, though nothing was said about this to

Tippoo Tib, to keep a watch on his supposed
superior.

Such was the political side of the treaty, which
had to be settled in order to afford a basis for the
second, the commercial one, which was much more
important to Stanley's present enterprise. Through
all his scientific and political undertakings he had
always remained a good man of business, and as
such let it be known that Emin was presumably in
possession of some 75 tons of ivory, which at a low
computation represented a value of about £10,000.
Tippoo Tib was to provide the carriers necessary to
convey this ivory to the coast, and thus cover most
of the cost of the expedition. These were further
to serve the purpose of conveying the ammunition
intended for Emin's relief from the Congo to the
Albert Nyanza.

The two high contracting parties, after long
haggling, agreed that Tippoo Tib should furnish
600 carriers, for whom he was to get £6 per head
for the journey from Stanley Falls to the lake and
back. Stanley, on his part, pledged himself to
secure Tippoo Tib and ninety-six followers free
passage to the Congo, including provisions, and to
conduct the caravan from there on to Stanley Falls.

After a farewell visit to the Sultan, productive of
many presents to both travellers, the *Madura* put to
sea on February 25, 1887. At Cape Town, where
they put in, Tippoo Tib had for the first time an
opportunity of making acquaintance with a European
town. The impression was, according to Stanley,
so tremendous that he declared he was now beginning to admire Europeans. So far he had regarded

them all as more or less fools, but now he realized that
they were far superior to the Arabs. To Stanley's
proposal that he should come with him some day to
London, and there make acquaintance with the
Europeans and their works at the fountain-head, he
answered, like a good Moslem, with the pious words,
' In sha Allah ' (if God wills), ' I shall go there.'
And there it has been left until to-day. His means
would have long since allowed of his making a
voyage to ' Ulaia,'* but, notwithstanding all the
offers made him, he has never got further than
being ready to go. Allah has not yet willed it.

On March 18 the *Madura* reached the mouth of
the Congo. The prospects of the voyage up the
river were very unfavourable, as the steamers expected were not available. At length they succeeded in chartering some craft, which next day
conveyed the expedition to Matadi, a spot 110
miles from the mouth. From there, owing to the
rapids, they had to march on foot. In a dis-
contented mood, due mainly to disputes between
the various tribes composing the caravan, they proceeded on March 21 towards Leopoldville, which
was reached on April 21. Here the difficulties as
to procuring steamers were repeated, but at last
they succeeded in shipping the whole expedition.
But the vessels proved so defective that on May 12,
at Bolobo, it became necessary to divide the caravan
into two parts. The advance column, consisting of
the healthiest men, under Stanley's personal leadership, was to sail up the Congo and Aruwimi as

* ' Ulaia,' from the Arabic ' Vilaje,' is the Swahili expression
for Europe.

far as Yambuya, and from there, as speed was
necessary, at once to take the land route eastwards
to the Albert Nyanza. As soon as they were dis-
embarked, the fastest of the steamers was to turn back
and pick up the rear column at Bolobo. According
to Stanley's reckoning, they also could reach Yambuya within six weeks, and there they were to take
over the loads left behind, which were to be conveyed by the carriers Tippoo Tib was to supply,
and follow the advance column as quickly as
possible.

This division of the expedition into two parts
was the prelude to very tragic events, which ended
in the almost total loss of the rear column.

Attached to it were five Englishmen : (1) Major
Barttelot, 'a generous, frank, and chivalrous young
officer, distinguished in Afghanistan and on the
Sudanese Nile for pluck and performance of duty'*;
(2) his friend, a young civilian named Jameson, a
gentleman of wealth with a passion for natural history
studies, whose alacrity, capacity, and willingness to
work were reported to be 'unbounded'; (3) Herbert
Ward, mentioned in the previous chapter, who had
long worked in Borneo, New Zealand, and the
Congo country, and was spoken of as bright, intelligent, and capable ; (4) John Rose Troup, who had
proved himself 'an industrious and zealous officer'
under Stanley in the Congo State ; and (5) William
Bonny, who had seen service in the Zulu and Nile
campaigns, and was reputed 'a staid and observing
man.'

The first-named was in all respects marked out

* *Cf.* 'In Darkest Africa,' vol. i., pp. 471-473.

for the chief command, a post for which, in Stanley's judgment, he was thoroughly suited. Jameson was to be second to him, and to take his place in case he was incapacitated.

On June 16 Stanley arrived at Yambuya, Barttelot having parted with him on the way to escort Tippoo Tib in a special steamer to his old station. The latter reports as follows :

'At last we came to the River Usoko, which higher up is called Mature. Stanley turned aside with all his boats towards the places where many of my men had been killed when they were marching with Salum bin Muhammed. His caravan now proceeded by that river with the steamboats. They gave the Major and me a boat to bring us to Stanley Falls. So we came to that place. And I had asked Stanley for powder, so that I might arm the 500 men whom I was to provide, if I could get them ; but he said : "I cannot spare you any of the powder I have, but buy some there at Stanley Falls." I had also got Belgian flags, which I was to hoist everywhere in the districts which I ruled. I hoisted one at Stanley Falls when I arrived, and there on the Usoko my men hoisted the flag wherever they came. At Stanley Falls I ran it up on a mast. The Major departed, and we took leave of each other.'

On June 25 Barttelot reached Yambuya, and on the 28th Stanley began his rapid advance to the Albert Nyanza. Before leaving he delivered to the commander of the rearguard the following instructions :*

* 'In Darkest Africa,' vol. i., p. 114.

' *June 24th*, 1887.

' *To Major Barttelot, etc.*

' SIR,

' As the senior of those officers accompanying me on the Emin Pasha Relief Expedition, the command of this important post naturally devolves on you. It is also for the interest of the Expedition that you accept this command, from the fact that your Sudanese company, being only soldiers and more capable of garrison duty than the Zanzibaris, will be better utilized than on the road.

' The steamer *Stanley* left Yambuya on the 22nd of this month for Stanley Pool. If she meets with no mischance she ought to be at Leopoldville on the 2nd of July. In two days more she will be loaded with about 500 loads of our goods, which were left in charge of Mr. J. R. Troup. This gentleman will embark, and on the 4th of July I assume that the *Stanley* will commence her ascent of the river, and arrive at Bolobo on the 9th. Fuel being ready, the 125 men in charge of Messrs. Ward and Bonny, now at Bolobo, will embark, and the steamer will continue her journey. She will be at Bangala on the 19th of July, and arrive here on the 31st of July. Of course, the lowness of the river in that month may delay her a few days, but, having great confidence in her captain, you may certainly expect her before the 10th of August.

' It is the non-arrival of these goods and men which compel me to appoint you as commander of this post. But as I shall shortly expect the arrival of a strong reinforcement of men, greatly exceeding the advance force, which must, at all hazards, push on to the rescue of Emin Pasha, I hope you will not be detained longer than a few days after the departure of the *Stanley* on her final return to Stanley Pool in August.

' Meantime, pending the arrival of our men and goods, it behoves you to be very alert and wary in the command of this stockaded camp. Though the camp is favourably situated and naturally strong, a brave enemy would find it no difficult task to capture if the commander is lax in discipline, vigour, and energy. Therefore I feel sure that I have made a wise choice in selecting you to guard our interests here during our absence.

' The interests now entrusted to you are of vital importance to this Expedition. The men you will eventually have under you consist of more than an entire third of the Expedition. The goods that will be brought up are the currency needed for transit through the regions beyond the lakes; there will be a vast store of ammunition and provisions, which are of equal importance to us. The loss of these men and goods would be certain ruin to us, and the advance force itself would need to solicit relief in its turn. Therefore, weighing this matter well, I hope you will spare no pains to maintain order and discipline in your camp, and make your defences complete and keep them in such a condition that, however brave an enemy may be, he can make no impression on them. For this latter purpose I would recommend you to make an artificial ditch 6 feet wide, 3 feet deep, leading from the natural ditch, where the spring is round the stockade. A platform, like that on the southern side of the camp, constructed near the eastern as well as the western gate, would be of advantage to the strength of the camp. For remember, it is not the natives alone who may wish to assail you, but the Arabs and their followers may, through some cause or other, quarrel with you and assail your camp.

'Our course from here will be due east, or by magnetic compass east by south as near as possible. Certain marches that we may make may not exactly lead in the direction aimed at. Nevertheless, it is the south-west corner of Lake Albert, near or at Kavalli, that is our destination. When we arrive there we shall form a strong camp in the neighbourhood, launch our boat, and steer for Kibero, in Unyoro, to hear from Signor Casati, if he is there, of the condition of Emin Pasha. If the latter is alive, and in the neighbourhood of the lake, we shall communicate with him, and our after conduct must be guided by what we shall learn of the intentions of Emin Pasha. We may assume that we shall not be longer than a fortnight with him before deciding on our return towards the camp along the same road traversed by us.

'We will endeavour, by blazing trees and cutting saplings along our road, to leave sufficient traces of the route taken by us. We shall always take, by preference, tracks leading eastward. At all crossings where paths intersect we shall hoe up and make a hole a few inches deep across all paths not used by us, besides blazing trees when possible.

'It may happen, should Tippu-Tib have sent the full number of adults promised by him to me, viz., 600 men (able to carry loads), and the *Stanley* has arrived safely with the 125 men left by me at Bolobo, that you will feel yourself sufficiently competent to march the column, with all the goods brought by the *Stanley* and those left by me at Yambuya, along the road pursued by me. In that event, which would be very desirable, you will follow closely our route, and before many days we should most assuredly meet. No doubt you will find our *bomas* intact and standing, and you should endeavour to make your marches so that you could utilize these as you marched. Better guides than those *bomas* of our route could not be made. If you do not meet them in the course of two days' march you may rest assured that you are not on our route.

'It may happen, also, that though Tippu-Tib has sent some men, he has not sent enough to carry the goods with your own force. In that case you will, of course, use your discretion as to what goods you can dispense with to enable you to march. For this purpose you should study your list attentively.

'1. Ammunition, especially fixed, is most important.

'2. Beads, brass wire, cowries and cloth, rank next.

'3. Private luggage.

'4. Powder and caps.

'5. European provisions.

'6. Brass rods as used on the Congo.

'7. Provisions (rice, beans, peas, millet, biscuits).

'Therefore you must consider, after rope, sacking, tools, such as shovels (never discard an axe or bill-hook), how many sacks of provisions you can distribute among your men to enable you to march—whether half your brass rods in the boxes could not go also and there stop. If you still cannot march, then it would be better to make two marches of six miles twice over if you prefer marching to staying for our arrival, than throw too many things away.

'With the *Stanley's* final departure from Yambuya you should not fail to send a report to Mr. William Mackinnon, c/o Gray, Dawes and Co., 13, Austin Friars, London, of what has happened at your camp in my absence, or when I started away eastward; whether you have heard of or from me at all, when you do expect to hear, and what you purpose doing. You should also send him a true copy of this order, that the Relief Committee may judge for themselves whether you have acted, or purpose to act, judiciously.

'Your present garrison shall consist of 80 rifles and from 40 to 50 supernumeraries. The *Stanley* is to bring you within a few weeks 50 more rifles and 75 supernumeraries, under Messrs. Troup, Ward, and Bonny.

'I associate Mr. J. S. Jameson with you at present. Messrs. Troup, Ward, and Bonny will submit to your authority. In the ordinary duties of the defence and the conduct of the camp or of the march there is only one chief, which is yourself; but, should any vital step be proposed to be taken, I beg you will take the voice of Mr. Jameson also. And when Messrs. Troup and Ward are here, pray admit them to your confidence, and let them speak freely their opinions.

'I think I have written very clearly upon everything that strikes me as necessary. Your treatment of the natives, I suggest, should depend entirely upon their conduct to you. Suffer them to return to the neighbouring villages in peace, and if you can in any manner by moderation, small gifts occasionally of brass rods, etc., hasten an amicable intercourse, I should recommend you doing so. Lose no opportunity of obtaining all kinds of information respecting the natives, the position of the various villages in your neighbourhood, etc.

'I have the honour to be,
'Your obedient servant,
'HENRY M. STANLEY,
'*Commanding Expedition.*'

The pith and marrow of the directions was that, whatever happened, the rear column was to follow the advance as quickly as possible. Stanley had thought it quite within the range of possibility that Tippoo Tib would either fail to furnish the promised carriers or else not supply enough, and he had fully discussed

Tippoo Tib's reliability with Barttelot after giving the latter his instructions. If this discussion took place as Stanley describes, it was clearly pointed out in the course of it that absolute reliance could not be placed on the Arab. The attempt to make a friend of him was a counsel of necessity, for without his goodwill, after the conflicts that had preceded between the Arabs and Belgians, a march through the districts to be traversed was impossible. But it was *a priori* doubtful whether, when brought within range of the influence of his revengeful fellow-tribesmen, he would carry out all the obligations he had undertaken, and still more uncertain after the disputes that had taken place between the European members of the caravan and Tippoo Tib's followers, particularly his puffed-up nephew, Salum bin Muhammed.

Beside this, Tippoo Tib had made Barttelot almost impossible promises at parting. He had said that he would despatch the 600 men he had engaged to supply within nine days. Stanley, who knew what the promises of Orientals were, saw at once that he would not do so. The Muhammedan, when speaking of anything he is going to do in the future, always adds, 'In sha Allah.' If he does not do it, it is just because God has not willed it. When Barttelot, in answer to Stanley's warnings, asked in perplexity why on earth they had had anything to do with the untrustworthy old campaigner, the wily American compared his Arab friend to the Maxim gun he had with him, which, so long as it worked properly, could do very good service, and was then of inestimable value. But it might happen to break down, owing to defective construction, wrong handling, or being tampered with by the enemy. In that case one had to trust to the rifles, which one also carried. Just so Tippoo Tib, if he did not fail through his own falseness, unskilful handling, or hostile influence, would be most helpful to the column. But, if he should be faithless, other resources must be forthcoming; and these in this case were his own men, who were with the rearguard, or whom, if necessary, they would enlist on their own account.

Stanley's forebodings were only too terribly realized. Tippoo Tib did indeed soon send off 500 men, but they only got as far as the mouth of the Aruwimi. That is just the spot where some years before Salum bin Muhammed's caravan had been massacred. This led their leader, Ali bin Muhammed, at once to start on a mock punitive expedition. He blazed away all his powder, did not dare go any further, and went back to Stanley Falls. This first attempt to obtain carriers was followed by various others. The officers of the rear column were constantly travelling to and fro between Yambuya, Stanley Falls, and Kassongo in search of Tippoo Tib, whose own concerns took him now here, now there, to hold him to the fulfilment of his agreement.

It must not be assumed that he had maliciously neglected his engagements, as Stanley tries to make out. He had already shown his good intentions by getting ready in a remarkably short time 500 carriers, for whose non-arrival he was not directly to blame. Even if gross neglect could be brought

home to him, there is much to be said in his
defence. The supplying of carriers had not been
made a primary stipulation of his engagement. He
was first and foremost Governor of the Stanley
Falls district, and, as such, had manifold duties,
which called him this way and that. To-day he
had to administer justice at Kassongo, to-morrow
to suppress disorders on the Lomami. In addition
to this, he was a merchant, and his mercantile
concerns naturally were more to him than the
success of Stanley, towards whom he felt himself
exonerated after having once supplied 500 men.
And he had obviously no inducement whatever
to do anything extra for Stanley when his own
experiences as to Stanley's promises are recol-
lected.

The moral responsibility for the tragic fate of
the rear column cannot in any way be imputed to
Tippoo Tib. First and foremost it falls on Stanley
himself, who left behind a large number of his
comrades under conditions the difficulties of which
he knew and with which they showed themselves
unable to cope. Next, the Europeans in charge of
the rear column must be pronounced to have shown
themselves quite incompetent, in face of those difficulties, when they arose. In the instructions given
by Stanley the event of the carriers not being
supplied had been expressly provided for. Should
it so happen, the rear column was to endeavour, as
best it could, to get on without outside assistance,
and to follow by quite short marches. This was
plainly laid down. Instead of this Barttelot let
a whole year pass, during which the greater part

of his men, who at a pinch could have made the
journey alone, perished miserably.

At last he had collected a number of carriers
which seemed to him sufficient, and decided on a
start on June 14, 1888. In forty-three days' march
the caravan covered ninety miles, to the village of
Banalya, a station of Tippoo Tib's, in charge of an
Arab named Abdallah Karoni. With him the Major
quarrelled, and so determined to journey back once
more to Stanley Falls, which he had visited seven
times in the course of the year, and complain to
Tippoo Tib. But he never lived to do so. On the
morning of July 19 he was treacherously shot by a
Manyema named Senga, whose wife he had told to
stop making a noise. For a moment it seemed as
if this was to be the signal for a general mutiny,
but Bonny, the only Englishman still with the
caravan, succeeded in mastering the excitement,
though he could not prevent several loads being
plundered.

Three days later Jameson came up with the last
of the stragglers. According to the instructions, he
was now to take over the command. In order to
make himself quite secure for the future, he determined to induce Tippoo Tib himself, by the offer of
a large sum of money, to lead the caravan on to the
Albert Nyanza, and for that purpose he betook
himself again to Stanley Falls. His arrival there
and his negotiations with Tippoo Tib are described
as follows in the autobiography :

'After a month Jameson appeared and announced
that the Major had been shot. His murderer was
Senga, who, however, had escaped. Some other

men too had fled, and about ten loads were missing. " But," he went on, " all the rest of the loads we have got together under guard at a place where there are townships near at hand, and all the rest of the people are there. And now I have come to ask you to accompany me." That meant myself and theBelgians. We asked him: "Why did Senga shoot the Major ?" He replied : " Because he forbade him to get up a *ngoma*. And his *wanyampara** said : ' This *ngoma* is for joy at our starting. Is it right for us to be mournful, as at a funeral ?' Then one evening between eight and nine the wives of Senga were singing, when the Major suddenly came and made passes with a spear at one of them. When her husband saw that, he fired at him. That is the reason." After four days they brought Senga and his wives and children in irons. I handed them over to the Belgians, and they asked him : " Why did you shoot the Major ?" He replied in the same way as Jameson had told us. They said : " If anyone set you on, say so, for you will be executed anyhow." But he replied : " No one set me on ; nor was there any other reason than what I have told you." Then the Belgians called me and Jameson, told us what Senga had said, and gave him up to Jameson. The latter ordered his execution. " But his belongings," he said, " are not implicated or to blame." So our slave Senga was shot.

' Jameson begged me to accompany him, but the Belgians said : " Hamid bin Muhammed must not go away. He is here in the service of the State, and

* Overseers of the caravan.

we are under him, so how can he go away? It
is in his agreement that he should give you men,
but not that he is to go with you himself." Then
Jameson promised to pay 50,000 to 60,000 dollars,
offering to pay it out of his own money if they
would not give it in Europe. But the Belgians
answered him : " If you want Hamed bin Muhammed, go to Banana and telegraph. If he gets leave
to conduct you, you can afterwards agree on his
salary." '

Thereupon Jameson determined to ask at Brussels
by telegraph, and proceeded down the river to hand
in the despatch himself. But he only got as far as
the Lomami, where he fell ill of fever and died.
Of the remaining Europeans belonging to the
expedition, Troup had been sent back to Europe
very ill, while Ward had apparently had differences
of opinion with the Major, and while waiting for
the telegraphic instructions of the home Committee
kept far away from the caravan on the Lower Congo.

The native portion of the rear column, now under
Bonny's command, had also shrunk to half its
numbers through illness and privation. In this
woeful plight did Stanley find his reserve, on which
he had built such great hopes, when he returned
from the Albert Nyanza to Banalya on August 17,
1888. After a most arduous march he had safely
joined the Pasha, on April 29, at Kawalli, on the
west shore of Albert Nyanza, and, after convincing
himself that no danger threatened him for the
moment, returned on June 1 to pick up the
remainder of the expedition, left behind a year
before on the Aruwimi.

Being now sufficiently provided with carriers, he returned on January 18, 1889, to the Albert Nyanza, and conducted the Pasha, who was very reluctant to abandon his post, half against his will, to the East Coast, which he reached—at Bagamoyo—on December 4. It is well known how Emin, who for more than ten years had braved the dangers of Central Africa, almost lost his life there by an accident. At a banquet given in his honour, the day after his arrival, by the German officials, owing to his shortsightedness, he fell out of the window, and sustained a fracture of the skull, which kept him for a long time on a sick bed. On recovering, he entered the service of the new German colony as Imperial Commissioner.

CHAPTER XV

'The old falls down, and time gives way to change,
And a new life arises from the ruins.'

SCHILLER : *Tell.*

WHEN Stanley returned to Banalya in August, 1888,
he at once wrote to Tippoo Tib, inviting him to
a conference. He, however, could not get away
himself, and sent in his stead his nephew, Salum
bin Muhammed, to confer with the explorer. Stanley
devotes several pages of his work to their interview,
but what he wanted of Tippoo Tib is not very clear.
On the one hand, he demanded that the Arab chief
should pay him back the passage of himself and his
men from Zanzibar to Stanley Falls, and replace all
goods that had been lost, threatening, if necessary, to enforce his claims with the help of the
Sultan and the British Consul-General; on the
other, a fresh contract seems to be again floating
before his eyes, which he evidently expects to
obtain cheaply by putting these demands forward.

Tippoo Tib, however, refused to be intimidated
by any threats, and remained in conscious innocence at his station, which of late had advanced

mightily as a centre of trade. ' Every month came Europeans to the camp in two or three boats, and they all took ivory on board—often they had to leave some behind. Stanley Falls was quite full of Europeans, and all that you could wish for was to be had there. It was a great port, and everything that one desired was to be had. Belgian and French trading companies also came there, and everywhere flourishing towns arose. And every boat that came took on board ivory.

' And it was at Stanley Falls as on the coast. No one sent for anything from Zanzibar, or Tabora, or Ujiji; everything was to be procured on the spot.'

With the Europeans, especially the Belgians, Tippoo Tib lived on the best of terms. Once the Governor himself visited him to discuss the fixing of an ivory tax. Our chronicler declares that the Congo State demanded a payment in kind of 5 pounds on every *frasila* (somewhat more than 14 per cent.). Tippoo Tib agreed to this for his own ivory, but requested that only 3 pounds (about 9 per cent.) should be levied from the other Arabs. The request was granted, and the Arabs agreed to the arrangement.

I have found no mention elsewhere of any such arrangement for taxing Tippoo Tib higher than other Arabs; but, as a fact, about the time he was Vali at Stanley Falls a tax in kind of 4 pounds was imposed. It is not impossible that, to make his fellow-tribesmen better disposed to the tax, he allowed himself to be treated less favourably, and procured them some mitigation. He eventually found ways and means to make his account out of it.

While he was thus attending to his duties in the
service of a European Power, he received from home
the news that his old patron, Seyyid Burghash, was
dead. He had long been suffering, and ended his
eventful life on March 27, 1888. The physical
troubles which made his last years a burden were,
however, trifling compared with the spiritual sufferings which darkened the evening of his life.

Burghash, as is well known, in 1870 ascended
the throne of his father, left vacant by the eagerly
expected death of his brother Majid. Like the
former, the type of an aristocratic Arab and an
Oriental despot from head to foot, he once more
revived for his country the days of ancient splendour,
which seemed to have been buried on the death of
Said. The forays of his subjects into the dark
interior, which he followed with interest and supported to the best of his power, brought rich
treasures into the country, of which he took his
share by levying considerable taxes. On the island
itself agriculture, especially the cultivation of the
clove, was in its fullest prosperity, and the Sultan
did not content himself with the produce of his own
plantations, but also laid a heavy tax on the crops
of his subjects; 30 per cent. of all cloves had to
be given over to him. He was also a keen man
of business, and had a whole fleet of merchant ships
afloat on the Indian Ocean.

The ample means thus obtained enabled him to
display the pomp worthy of an Eastern Prince. The
palace which he built for himself, and which still
serves as a residence for his successor, is known,
on account of its extravagant furnishing, as *Bet el*

Ajaib, or the 'House of Wonders.' Numerous country houses, situated in the most beautiful parts of the island and still favourite resorts, are also his work. He not only shone in outward splendour, but, like a wise ruler, applied the treasures that came flowing to him to further the welfare of his subjects. He raised himself a lasting memorial by the construction of a magnificent aqueduct. From Khemkhen, an abundant spring to the north of the town, he brought down excellent drinking-water through miles of pipes, which may be drawn to this day by every inhabitant of Zanzibar, free of cost, from numberless fountains.

The days of power and splendour soon went by. The Europeans, who till now had stayed in the country as peaceful traders or journeyed into the interior as harmless explorers, began to become politically dangerous, and hence the events which we have already touched on in Chapter XII. Towards the close of his life Burghash had lost his possessions on the mainland, and the time was not far distant when the land of his fathers would fall wholly under Western control.

The news of Burghash's death was received by Tippoo Tib via Europe, to which it had been telegraphed—another sign how the times had changed. Two decades before he, like so many of his compatriots, had set out from the East Coast, not knowing how the road would end, and, cut off for years from communication with home, had pressed further and further towards the west. Now the Westerners had advanced from the same quarter into the wilderness, whose depths he had pene-

trated, and there, with the superior discoveries of
their genius, had secured the sovereignty for themselves. Their steamers plied on the African river
which had been awaked from its sleep of thousands
of years, and brought the furthest strongholds of
the Arab slave-hunters into communication with
European civilization.

Tippoo Tib, who was always in favour of good
relations with his rulers, at once sent to Burghash's
successor, his brother Khalifa, an embassy to convey
congratulations to him on his accession to the
throne, and assure him of the allegiance of his
influential subject. Tippoo Tib's son Sef had
shortly before set out for the coast, and could still
be overtaken by couriers and instructed to appear
as his father's spokesman before the new Sultan.

But our hero himself was soon warned in an
unpleasant manner to return to Zanzibar. The
King of the Belgians informed him that Stanley had
made serious accusations against him. He was said
to be guilty of the death of Major Barttelot, and by
the breach of the duties he had undertaken by
agreement with Stanley to have caused material
damage to the expedition led by the latter;
Stanley had cited him before the English court at
Zanzibar; a great lawsuit was in prospect, and his
property there had already been sequestrated. A
legal summons would probably reach him shortly.

This news startled Tippoo Tib out of his calm,
and he at once determined to travel to Zanzibar to
defend himself against the accusations raised against
him. In March, 1890, he started, after having taken
a most friendly leave of the Europeans at his station.

Rashid, the son of his cousin and companion in arms Bwana Nzige, was made Vali in his place, while two Arab friends were to look after his commercial interests during his absence.

His fellow-tribesmen at Stanley Falls endeavoured in every possible way to hold back Tippoo Tib from making the journey to the coast; they feared that it might go ill with him before the judgment-seat of the Europeans. In the old familiar places, too, which he passed through—Nyangwe and Kassongo —the worst was prophesied, and he was advised rather to let all his property in Zanzibar go, and to enjoy his life here among his friends, far beyond the reach of the arm of the law. He had quite sufficient fortune left in the interior to live comfortably.

But Tippoo Tib, in his superior wisdom, flung all these well-meant warnings to the winds. To begin with, he felt himself innocent, and thought he would be able to prove it on the coast. Secondly, he said to himself that, if the decision should really go against him, as things then stood he would not be safe from the vengeance of the Europeans, even in the farthest depths of the interior. Whom should he call to his aid against the firearms of the white men? What sort of warriors the Manyema were he had learnt years before, when with a handful of riflemen he conquered the tribes one after another, divided as they were by internal dissensions. He had meanwhile seen with his own eyes the superior power of the Europeans, and knew that nothing could be done against them with such undisciplined savages as he had at command.

He seems to have been very outspoken with the Arabs who were besetting him, and flung about him such expressions as 'nonsense' and 'silly fools.'

When even his friend Bwana Nzige urged him to resist the Europeans, his patience gave way altogether, and he rejoined quite tragically : 'Do you, too, speak in this wise ? I always took you for a sensible man, and now you talk like that !'

On his way to Tanganyika, Tippoo Tib met Msabbah bin Njem, the Vali of that district, by whom he was told that Rumalisa, whose headquarters were at Ujiji, was arming to attack the Europeans west of the lake. Captain Jaques had started on an expedition thither for the Belgian Anti-slavery Society, and all Arab slave-traders felt their most particular interests threatened by his appearance. It was easy for Rumalisa, with the hatred towards Europeans which, even apart from this provocation, was seething in them, to find numerous adherents for his hostile plans.

Tippoo Tib had heard before this of the intentions of his vassal, and had energetically enjoined on him to refrain from all hostilities. In Mtoa he met him, and learned to his delight that nothing had come of the purposed attack. Rumalisa had indeed, in defiance of the commands of Tippoo Tib, made all preparations for fighting ; but the boat that was to bring the necessary powder across Tanganyika luckily let in the water, and so he was forced to abstain from a struggle which would have damaged the interests of the Arabs at least as much as those of the Belgians. Later on, when Tippoo Tib was out of the country, Rumalisa renewed the abortive attack, and by so doing initiated a period of severe conflicts, in which much blood was shed, and in the end the power of his fellow-tribesmen was totally broken.

Tippoo Tib, who still considered himself in the service of the King of the Belgians, in accordance with the instructions he had received hoisted the blue flag with the golden star, then crossed Tanganyika, and marched from Ujiji towards the home of his fathers, Tabora.

On the way he received letters from Zanzibar, among them the summons from the court already announced. Stanley had brought an action for 90,000 dollars (about £11,000) damages, and the English judge, Cracknall, informed him that unless he put in an appearance before the court within six months, judgment would be given against him.

A curious item in this summons was the fact that the Arabic text gave as plaintiffs ' Emin Pasha and his people,' of course meaning the Relief Committee. In any case the wording was calculated to bring about misunderstandings, and the Pasha, as soon as he learned the misuse of his name, issued a public declaration stating that he had nothing whatever to do with the suit ; that, on the contrary, he had parted with Tippoo Tib's people, who had escorted him to the coast, on the best of terms. This declaration was sent in print to all Arabs of consequence in Zanzibar, and a document of similar tenour was sent to Tippoo Tib as well.

Emin Pasha was known to all those who had become intimate with him as particularly touchy, and had often shown plainly that he was capable of being seriously aggrieved over the veriest trifles. In this case, however, more was at issue. He had just entered the service of the German Empire, and was on the point of beginning a long journey to the interior. When it was made to appear through the summons, read with interest by all Arabs, that he was at grievous feud with Tippoo Tib, the uncrowned ruler of Central Africa, he had reason to expect the greatest hindrances on his journey, and so it is not to be wondered at that he did all he could to set right erroneous surmises which might attach to the wording of that summons.

That the English judge purposely designated the plaintiffs so ambiguously can scarcely be conceived, although to the end of his life he was a deadly hater of Germans and was no well-wisher of Emin. At all events, when his attention was drawn to the doubtfulness of the wording, he did nothing to dispel any doubts that might attach to it.

At Unyanyembe Tippoo Tib could feel himself once more at home. His old friend Mirambo had indeed been dead some years, and his brother, who succeeded him, Mpanda Sharo, had also died meanwhile. The present ruler was a son of Mirambo's, who kept up the old friendship of his father for Tippoo Tib, and received him respectfully, as his father would have done. At the English mission-house near Tabora a hospitable reception was also accorded him.

The changes which our hero this time found on his return in his native district were far greater than those which met his eyes on his previous visit. In order to depict them we must connect them with

the events at which we broke off in Chapter XII.
—the historical description of the German acquisitions in East Africa.

In April, 1888, Seyyid Khalifa signed the treaty by which the coast of our present colony was leased out to the German East African Company. Besides the control of the Customs, all the sovereign rights hitherto exercised by the Sultan, especially that of justice, were transferred to the Company, which, as an external mark of its power, hoisted its own flag at all the places it occupied beside the red banner of the Sultan. In spite of the artistic design of the flag, which, in addition to the German colours, bears the Southern Cross as a crest—this outward act of 'taking seisin' was not at once followed by the actual subjugation of the territory ceded.

The native population from the first viewed their new masters with distrust. What was said before about the behaviour of the Tabora Arabs to the German merchants was here, in an increased degree, true of the whole population of the coast as regards the officials of the Company. To the jealousy of competition was added the fear of ere long falling wholly under the sway of the Europeans, who, according to their view, would put a stop to much that hitherto had been a matter of course : in the first place, the slave-trade, by which, directly or indirectly, almost the whole population lived—the Arabs and Swahilis by going out on raids and making profit out of the sale of the slaves carried off, the Indians by supplying at a high price the powder necessary for these expeditions and advancing the other goods needed for such enterprises at a high rate of interest.

The discontent which was fermenting in all was easily stirred up by those elements, which had most to lose if greater order became generally prevalent. Among these were, above all, the many officials of the Sultan who had hitherto drawn a comfortable extra income from bribes and cheating the Customs, and saw themselves suddenly robbed of it. Then there were the local chiefs who had unconditionally recognised the overlordship of the Sultan, and now felt themselves threatened by the foreigners settled on the coast; these, too, were easily induced to join movement against the interlopers. A convenient incitement in the universal indignation was religion, indifferent as the East African generally is to his soul's welfare. It was also alleged that the officers of the Company did not always show tact in dealing with the natives. They were mostly young and placed among unfamiliar conditions, so that blunders were likely to occur. Yet it may be confidently asserted that even the wisest and most temperate conduct would not have checked the movement.

The Sultan, who had only agreed to the coast treaty under compulsion, did nothing to quiet the disturbed spirits ; on the contrary, he undoubtedly regarded the incipient hostilities with complacency, and as far as lay in his power supported the resistance* of the people of the coast to the new element.

* Cf. for what follows Rochus Schmidt, 'Geschichte des Araberaufstandes in Ostafrika.'

The first open resistance was offered in August, 1888, at Pangani, where the Sultan's Vali tried to prevent the hoisting of the Company's flag. The appearance of two men-of-war, the *Möwe* and the *Carola*, restored tranquillity for the time being; but hardly were they gone when the two officers of the Company were made prisoners in their own house by the natives, and were only saved with difficulty by the intervention of the Englishman Mathews, the Sultan's well-known general and subsequently Prime Minister of Zanzibar. At Tanga and Bagamoyo also hostilities broke out in September. The soul of the rising was the Arab Bushir bin Salum el Harthi, who had won warlike fame in successful struggles with Mirambo, and even by armed resistance to Sultan Burghash. He also stirred up Bwana Heri, the influential Sultan of Useguha, the hinterland of Saadani, to resistance. The Company was quite powerless in face of the gathering rising; the German men-of-war could, of course, only intervene at the larger ports and were unable to enforce a lasting peace. Except Bagamoyo and Dar-es-salaam, the whole north coast had to be given up, and at the end of the year the south also fell to the rebels. At Lindi and Mikindani the officers of the Company, when all resistance seemed hopeless, were just barely able to save themselves, while at Kilwa two brave officials paid for their heroic defence of the post entrusted to them with their lives.

Meanwhile, people at home had recognized that if they did not mean wholly to give up the German cause in the new regions, the Empire must adopt energetic

measures. After brief negotiations with England
and Portugal, our neighbours in East Africa, it
was determined to blockade the entire coast between 10° 28′ and 2° 10′ of south latitude, so as to
prevent the importation of munitions of war. This
blockade was opened on December 2 by the
German and English admirals Deinhardt and Fre-
mantle. A further decisive step was taken when,
on January 30, 1889, the Reichstag adopted a Bill*
by which a sum of 2,000,000 marks was placed
at the disposal of the State for the effectual protection of German interests in East Africa, and it
was decided to entrust the carrying out of the
necessary measures to an Imperial Commissioner.

To this post, as we know, Captain Hermann
Wissmann was nominated. He had first made his
reputation as an explorer by crossing the Dark
Continent from west to east, as was mentioned in
Chapter X., and during the years 1883-1885 had
made successful journeys of exploration in the
Congo Basin, while an expedition at the end of that
year to the south of the newly-founded Congo State,
forced on him against his will by the attitude
of the Arabs, who were then at war with the
Belgians, had been prolonged into a second crossing of Africa. After having thus, with short
intervals, spent almost eight years of activity in
the interior, he returned home in the summer of
1888. He had then been selected, together with

---

* In order to secure a majority in the Reichstag, the question
of slavery was skilfully tacked to it. This secured the votes of
the Centre. The same tactics had been previously adopted by
Bismarck to force England to join in the blockade.

Dr. Peters, to lead the expedition planned by the Germans for the relief of Emin Pasha, but at the last moment it was still possible to secure him for the post of Commissioner.

The preparations for the suppression of the rising were made with the utmost speed. At Wissmann's suggestion, native African tribes were employed, under the command of German officers and non-commissioned officers. With the assent of the Egyptian Government, 700 Soudanese were enlisted, and, after negotiations with Portugal, 100 Zulus. The Europeans appointed were twenty-one officers (including surgeons and officials) and forty non-commissioned officers.

On March 21, 1889, Wissmann reached Zanzibar, and from there, after a short stay with the leader of the German squadron, Admiral Deinhardt, proceeded to the mainland. On April 28, after an agreement concluded with the principal representative of the German East African Company, M. de St. Paul Illaire, the entire control of the Company's territory, exclusive of the Customs, was handed over to the Imperial Commissioner. On April 29 the first transport, with the Soudanese, reached Bagamoyo. On May 6 all the fighting force was assembled, and then followed in rapid succession the warlike incidents by which the resistance of the rebels was gradually broken.

On May 8 Bushiri's fortified camp near Bagamoyo was stormed, though he himself unfortunately escaped. Bwana Heri's headquarters at Saadani, which had been previously bombarded by the naval force without definite result, fell on June 6. Pangani

15

fell on July 9, and about the same time Tanga was taken by the sailors. Meanwhile various attempts had been made to enter into peaceful negotiations with the rebels, but they led to no result. Sleman bin Nasor el Lemki, later well known in Europe as the Vali of Dar-es-Salaam, had been sent by the Commissioner to Pangani to treat with the Arabs there, but was received with musket shots and could not land. Tippoo Tib's son Sef also tried in vain to make himself useful. Coming from the interior, he had reached the coast near Saadani with a great caravan of ivory, and with Wissmann's permission had taken on his treasures to Zanzibar. At Wissmann's request, he returned to Saadani to induce Bwana Heri to accept peace, but was not successful.

When Bushiri saw his power broken on the coast he withdrew further into the interior and attacked the town of Mpapwa, where the German East African Company had a settlement. This he destroyed. Wissmann followed him with a large force, reached Mpapwa on October 10, and established there a fresh and strongly fortified station.

Bushiri meanwhile had made off again. He had found numerous adherents among the warlike Wahehe and Mafiti, and hastened now to make use of the Commissioner's absence for a fresh advance on the coast. He had already penetrated as far as Usaramo, and his hordes had there practised the most inhuman cruelties, when Wissmann's lieutenant, Freiherr von Gravenreuth, advanced against him from Dar-es-Salaam. Near the township of Yombo he inflicted a serious defeat on the insurgents, but

Bushiri again escaped. His auxiliaries, however, deserted him, and at length, after he had once more barely escaped with his life in an attack on the village of Masiro, Jumben Magaya succeeded in taking him prisoner at Kwa Mkoro, on the borders of Nguru. The chief, Dr. Schmidt, took him to Pangani, where he was hanged on December 15.

It now became necessary to break down the resistance of the powerful Bwana Heri, who was arming afresh in the hinterland of Saadani. A detachment sent out to reconnoitre under Rochus Schmidt on December 27 came unexpectedly at Mlembula on a strongly fortified *boma* in the bush, whose existence had hitherto been unknown. An attack on it was repulsed, whereupon Wissmann assembled all the fighting forces at his disposal for a fresh advance, and on January 3, 1890, after a furious conflict, stormed the stronghold, which proved itself a model of African fortification.

Bwana Heri escaped, and assembled his troops at Palamakaa, a village five hours' march from Saadani, for further resistance. There he held out for some time against various attacks, but at last, on March 9, was a second time defeated by Wissmann. Though it proved impossible to secure his person, his resistance was now broken. His ammunition and provisions were almost exhausted, so that he no longer showed himself inaccessible to the proposals of peace made him through Sleman bin Nasor. In April he formally submitted to the Commissioner, who forgave him the past, in the hope that his influence over the numerous natives he ruled might in the future further the German cause. Though this

15—2

hope was not realized in the long-run, it was of
great advantage at that critical time to have gained
him even as a temporary ally.

The winning back of the north soon followed the
reconquest of the south. The towns of Mikindani
and Sudi submitted voluntarily, and here again it
was Sleman bin Nasor who successfully conducted
the negotiations. The services which he rendered
to the German cause in those dark days should
never be forgotten. The ports of Kilwa and Lindi
were occupied early in May, after bombardment
from the sea, and received permanent garrisons. A
station was also established at Mikindani. The
suppression of the rising was thus complete, and at
the end of the month Wissmann was able to go
home on leave, so as to restore his health, which had
been sorely injured by fourteen months' continual
exertions.

In the meantime measures had been taken at
Berlin to secure international recognition for the
African territories just purchased with German
blood. As a supplement to the London Convention
of November 1, 1886, a new treaty was concluded
with England, by which the colonies of German and
British East Africa were constituted in their
present shape.

Great Britain undertook to exert all her influence
to induce the Sultan by friendly means to cede the
strip of coast still belonging to him for a reasonable
compensation. Germany in return recognised the
British protectorate over the possessions retained
by the Sultan, including Zanzibar and Pemba,
and left to British influence the territory of

Witu, to which Germany had acquired certain rights by compacts with its Sultan. The numerous claims renounced by Germany in Africa were compensated by the cession of the island of Heligoland. This British protectorate over the Sultan's territory was proclaimed on November 4, 1890.

As is well known, the compact was generally regarded as a heavy blow to our colonial policy. Above all, those who knew the conditions from their own observation regretted that we had left to the English the island of Zanzibar, which extended in front of our coast-line, and the city of the same name. It is no part of this work to criticize the provisions of that treaty, but this one fact should be pointed out—that at this day the port of Zanzibar commands the whole East African coast; that all the larger German firms, with the German East African Company and the German East African Line at their head, have their principal establishments there. Zanzibar must be of greater consequence to our coast than the island of Bornholm to the shores of the Baltic. This parallel was drawn in the pamphlet in defence of the Anglo-German agreement.

The amount of the compensation that the Sultan was to receive for the cession of the littoral was fixed by an exchange of notes between the German and British Governments at £200,000 in gold, payable in London by the expiration of the year 1890. The sum was raised by the German East African Company, which for this purpose, as well as for the necessary capital expenditure for agricultural purposes, received the privilege of issuing bonds to bearer to the amount of 10,556,000 marks. This was settled in an agreement on November 20, by which the relations between the Government and the Company were regulated. The chief stipulation of this compact was that from the date of payment of the indemnity the Company transferred all its sovereign rights obtained by treaty with the Sultan of Zanzibar to the Empire. The latter in turn undertook for a considerable number of years to pay the Company 600,000 marks annually out of the proceeds of the Customs, and granted it, in addition, a great number of proprietary rights.

In fulfilment of these stipulations, on January 1, 1891, the Empire took over the government of the newly-established colony, to which Freiherr von Soden, hitherto Governor of Cameroon, was appointed. On March 22 Wissmann's troops were transformed into Imperial Constabulary, while on July 1 the management of the Customs also passed into the hands of the Colonial Government.

After an orderly state of affairs had thus been established in the coastal districts, the question arose how to extend German influence further into the interior. To follow the various stages of this development lies outside the scope of our work ; we will content ourselves with briefly describing how Tippoo Tib's native land, Unyanyembe, was incorporated in the German dominions.

We have already mentioned that Emin, after recovering from his serious accident at Bagamoyo, placed his services at the disposal of the Imperial Government. On April 26, 1890, he set out from Bagamoyo with two officers (Langheld and Dr. Stuhlmann), two under-officers, 100 coloured soldiers,

and 400 armed carriers, to bring the district about
the lakes under German control. The intention
was to diverge from Mpapwa north-westward to the
Victoria Nyanza, without touching Tabora. This
was the express wish of Wissmann, who knew the
balance of power between the Arabs there from his
own observation, and was afraid that the appearance of Emin's comparatively slender force would
evoke unnecessary alarm, and so hinder a better-
equipped advance at a more convenient time.
Want of carriers, however, and the need of com-
pleting his articles of barter, forced the Pasha,
contrary to the original plan, to make for the Arab
entrepôt. The hostilities dreaded did not occur ; on
the contrary, before reaching Tabora Emin received
a missive from the Arabs begging him to hoist the
German flag in their town.

The victories of Wissmann over the insurgents
had naturally not remained unknown here in the
interior. Every native knew that the coast had fallen
into German hands, and also realized that if he fell
out with the masters of that coast all the treasures
that he had stored up at a distance would retain
little commercial value, and that whoever ventured along the accustomed homeward path in
defiance of the new rulers was simply throwing his
life away. Those who still wished to ignore these
facts had shortly before had their eyes opened by the
example of the murderer Muhammed bin Kasum.
Thus their own shrewdness bade the Arabs be on
good terms with the Germans. It happened very
fortunately, moreover, that an influential trader who
was devoted to Wissmann, the Beluchi Ismael, had

arrived at Tabora shortly before Emin. Thanks very largely to his powers of persuasion, the Arabs of their own accord solicited German protection. The only one who struggled energetically against the new sovereignty was the chief Sike, but even his opposition was at length broken down by the insistence of the Arabs.

On August 1 Emin hoisted the German flag at Tabora. He concluded a convention with the Arabs, in which they expressly acknowledged German rule in Unyanyembe, but were granted the right of choosing a Vali for themselves. They were unanimous in favour of the ' Besar ' Sef bin Saad, who afterwards, when a station was established at Tabora, submitted to its jurisdiction, and has filled the post assigned him by the confidence of his fellow-tribesmen to the satisfaction of the Colonial Government up to the present day.*

The new protectors were not long in want of opportunities for armed interference, in favour of their subjects. The marauding Wangoni were once more on the warpath, and had penetrated into the adjoining territory of Urambo. The German commander Freiherr von Bülow, who had joined the expedition from Mpapwa with twenty-five men, was sent to meet them, and at first tried to treat with the assailants. When this failed and the Wangoni only advanced in thicker swarms, he appealed to the Pasha for support, which he received in the shape of Lieutenant Langheld with seventy men, and marched against the enemy, with 2,000 Urambo men at his back as well. Four days' fighting

* Sef has since died.

(September 9 to 12) ended in the route of the Wangoni.

The Pasha had meanwhile marched off in the direction of the Victoria Nyanza, and Langheld, when the fight was over, sent his men after him, remaining behind himself to wait for a further expedition sent into the lake region under the Irishman Stokes and Lieutenant Sigl. Freiherr von Bülow remained for the present at Urambo. Here he was visited by Tippoo Tib, who had reached the territory of Unyanyembe shortly before the Pasha's departure. The Arabs, among whom Bülow seems to have been considered a particularly stern master, had indeed warned him against this visit, on the principle, 'Never go to your Prince when you are not summoned.' But the missionary who had received him so kindly, Dr. Shaw, known, on account of his lean little figure, by the name of Mzara Mkiuno,* had persuaded him that a man of his importance might venture into the lion's den. And Tippoo Tib went, and cannot find words to express his praise of the honourable reception prepared for him by the man to whom even the Vali of Tabora went with trembling. ' We asked each other after our health, and he offered me tea and coffee. When I left I pitched my camp at the watering-place near him. He sent me all sorts of things and seven oxen to make me quite content.'

Our hero is always happy when he can dilate as lengthily as possible on his good relations with Europeans, less in order to proclaim his loyalty than to display the diplomatic penetration with

* A Kinyamwezi expression, meaning ' hunger in the back.'

which he, first among his countrymen, recognized
the superior power of the Westerners and the value
of being on good terms with them.

As Bülow was recalled from his post soon after
Tippoo Tib's arrival, they determined to travel to
the coast together. But when all was prepared for
a start, Tippoo Tib was attacked by acute dysentery,
which stretched him for a long time on a bed of
sickness. For four months he hovered between life
and death, and it was only through the untiring care
of the White Fathers at Kipalapala that he eventually recovered. Scarcely had he recovered than
he set out to appear as soon as possible before the
English court. On the day after the Pilgrims'
Festival of 1308 (end of July, 1891) he left Tabora,
though still so weak that he had to be carried on a
litter. After two days he was just able to mount a
donkey. It is a remarkable fact, worthy of special
notice, that this was the first time that he had used
any animal for riding; his previous long journeys
had all been covered on foot.

At Mpapwa the missionaries told him a strange
story of his friend Stanley. He had, it appears,
spread the report in Europe that Jameson had
bought a girl slave at Yambuya, and in his presence
had her killed and devoured by the Manyema. The
story naturally evoked general indignation, and
Jameson's widow went herself with her brother-
in-law to Africa to collect on the spot proofs of
the groundlessness of the accusations made against
her late husband. While Mrs. Jameson remained
behind at Zanzibar, her brother-in-law equipped an
expedition to meet Tippoo Tib, and question him as

to what he knew of the matter. He turned back, however, at Mpapwa, presumably because he was by then fully convinced that the whole horrible story, by which his brother's good name had been endangered, was a malevolent fabrication.

Documentary evidence as to this episode is unhappily not at my disposal, but it is mentioned also by the well-known writer Henryk Sienkiewicz, who was staying at Zanzibar at the same time as Mrs. Jameson, in his 'Letters from Africa' (pp. 114 *et seq.*)—the silliest work, I may remark, that was ever written on African matters. He reports that Jameson had been universally condemned on the strength of Stanley's story, which was believed, and that the position of his widow in the English community was a most painful one.

Tippoo Tib was beside himself when he heard of these accusations, and gave vent to his feelings in the following terms : ' The story is a lie. I was not there, but neither saw nor heard anything of it till to-day among you. That he—Jameson—could do such a thing is absolutely impossible. Or do you think that I would tolerate such a thing? But I have never seen a European or any other being that could lie like this fellow. And how can the people judge whether he is lying?'

And he went on furiously soliloquizing : ' All the great kindnesses that I showed him were not enough for him—by way of thanks he wants to drown me now as well. I had a specimen in the promises that he made me : " When I get to Europe I do not know what I shall not give you, for I shall obtain boundless wealth and great influence." And he sent me his photograph! And when we met again he presented me at Cape Town with a dog. I at once passed it on to Jameson. It was a wretched little dog. I knew that he was a liar. No, it was not enough for him to malign me after his cheating. He maligned a dead man—Jameson—as well.'

On the further march through Usagara, Tippoo Tib received a letter from the Governor, inviting him to a consultation. He reached the coast at Bagamoyo, and was, as he again proudly mentions, received with high honour by the Head of the District, Schmidt. Then Freiherr von Soden came himself to fetch him to Dar-es-Salaam, the new capital. After he had stayed there a few days he crossed to Zanzibar.

The period appointed by the court had, of course, long since expired, but of all the threats that had been set forth in its summons none had come to pass. Stanley had failed in his accusations, and his own agent, the representative of Smith, Mackenzie and Co., invited Tippoo Tib to his house, where a joint document was signed, by which Tippoo Tib and Stanley withdrew their respective demands. The matter was thus finally settled. 'But few Europeans inquired about it, owing to Stanley's lies in the Jameson affair.'

CHAPTER XVI

COLLAPSE OF THE ARAB POWER

' As if whipped by invisible spirits, the sun-horses of Time
break away with the light chariot of our fate, and nothing is
left us but bravely and calmly to hold fast the reins, and guide
the wheels now right, now left, to avoid here a stone and there
an overthrow. Whither the way lies, who knows? He
scarcely remembers whence he came.'—GOETHE : *Egmont.*

SINCE that time Tippoo Tib has made no more
journeys to the interior ; he was spared the spectacle
of the complete collapse of the Arab power in the
districts he had ruled. As mentioned in the previous
chapter, Emin had on August 1 hoisted the German
flag at Tabora, and soon after Lieutenant Sigl established a permanent station there. His position was
not an easy one, for the Arabs, who at first readily
accepted the German domination, had been enraged
to the utmost by the news that the Pasha had
executed several of their countrymen on the Victoria
Nyanza, and through them the chief Sike, who
had only submitted unwillingly, was once more
encouraged to resistance.

As long as Sigl himself was head of the station
peace was at least outwardly preserved. After he
was relieved Sike proceeded to open hostilities. On
June 6, 1892, an attempt was made by Sigl's suc-

cessor, Dr. Schwesinger, with the aid of the anti-
slavery expedition under Count Schweinitz, which
was there at the time, to storm Quikuru, the chief's
boma; but it failed, and various subsequent engagements brought no decided success. At length, on
January 13, 1893, Lieutenant Prince succeeded, after
a fierce fight, in storming Sike's stronghold, when
the chief himself and many of his adherents lost their
lives by an explosion.

It is worthy of mention that during these conflicts Tippoo Tib's stepmother, Nyaso, constantly
showed herself well disposed towards the Germans ;
indeed, she actively supported the last decisive
assault by supplying eighty carriers.

Upon Sike's death the German rule in Tabora
was permanently established. Sigl, who soon afterwards again took over the control of the station,
could now proceed to extend our influence further
westward. The road to Tanganyika was by no
means secure, and complaints of the plundering of
caravans were still constantly coming in ; numerous
local chiefs were at feud with each other, and so
caused disorder in their own and the neighbouring
territories. To add to this came the announcement
that Muhammed bin Khalfan Rumalisa, the so-called
Vali of Ujiji, in the presence of a numerous gathering, had torn up and trampled upon a German
flag presented to him by Emin, with threats of
war to the knife against the Germans. He was
also suspected—with good reason, as it afterwards
proved—of having supported the rebel Sike with an
armed force shortly before the decisive encounter.
His troops, however, were surprised by natives on

their entry into Urambo; 200 men were slaughtered, and the rest took to flight.

The Wahehe, too, who on August 17, 1891, treacherously destroyed a strong expedition under von Zalewski, commander of the constabulary, were, according to Tippoo Tib's statements, supported by Rumalisa.

In order to take advantage as far as possible of the widespread impression produced by the defeat of Sike, Sigl determined to march at once to Tanganyika in person. He left Tabora on June 19, restored order everywhere on the way, reconciled various Sultans to the German rule, and reached Ujiji on July 24. A day's march short of that place the Arabs came to meet him and assure him of their loyalty. He hoisted the German flag at Ujiji, and set up Msabbah bin Nyem el Shehebi as Vali, with the consent of the inhabitants.

Rumalisa had thought it better not to await the arrival of the German leader. True, in numerous letters he had given expression to his unalterable friendship ; but he must have had a bad conscience with regard to his former intrigues, for, without informing his fellow-tribesmen, he crossed the lake in a small boat, and, as we shall see later, gave much trouble to the Belgians, whom no less than the Germans he regarded as his natural enemies.

This expedition of Sigl's effectively subdued the German sphere of interest as far as its extreme western frontier. Meanwhile the Belgians had not been idle in making their control a reality in all the districts reserved for them. In the south, during

the years 1891-1892, the expeditions of Stairs,
Delcommune, and Bia subjugated the territory of
Katanga ; in order to secure the north and north-
east as well, the explorer Van Kerkhove in 1890
made an expedition from Stanley Pool as far as the
frontier of Wadelai. On the upper Aruwimi he
had many conflicts with slave-stealers, on whom,
being provided with an excellent military equipment,
he inflicted crushing defeats. The tidings of them
roused the anger of the Arabs established on the
middle Congo, who were all more or less connected
with the traders, and felt that the damage done to
the latter in their calling must seriously affect themselves. Mwinyi Mohara, the head of the slave-
traders at Nyangwe, stirred up a general rising,
and at his instigation, in May, 1892, the European
Hodister, who lay with a trading expedition on the
Congo, south of Stanley Falls, was murdered. The
events that resulted from this act of violence, and
ended in the total collapse of the Arab power to the
west of Tanganyika as well, are thus described by
Tippoo Tib :

‘The Belgians, in order to avenge Hodister’s
death, called on Sef, who, as all knew, represented
his father at Stanley Falls, to take arms against
Mwinyi Mohara. Sef, who by open hostility towards
that influential slave- and ivory-trader would, of
course, have alienated all his fellow-tribesmen,
replied that he could not venture on such an important step without consulting his father. Thereupon the Belgians broke off the negotiations, and
came to terms with Ngongo Luteta.’

This man was, as may be remembered, a slave of

Tippoo Tib's, and had been placed by his master as his representative in his most especial domain of Utetera, between the Lomami and the Congo. After Tippoo Tib's departure from Stanley Falls, he became fairly independent, and ventured on various raids into the territory on the left bank of the Lomami. The Belgians, therefore, made war on him, and after he had been several times defeated, in the middle of 1892 he submitted to Commandant Dhanis, who then established a military post in the immediate neighbourhood of his chief town, Ngandu.

Sef—so Tippoo Tib declares—knew nothing of the peace between Ngongo Luteta and the Belgians. He was indignant that a vassal of his father's, after committing various other acts outside his prerogative, should have carried on war on his own account. He tried several times to induce Ngongo Luteta to give way, but the latter simply had Sef's messengers knocked on the head. Sef thus found himself compelled to advance in arms against the recalcitrant slave. Then, to his astonishment, the Belgians, towards whom he had no hostile intentions, suddenly intervened on behalf of Ngongo Luteta. He was thus forced into war with them against his will and simply through a misunderstanding.

So Tippoo Tib, cautiously as he expresses himself, throws the blame of beginning hostilities on the Belgians, who conspired with his vassal behind his son's back. It is hardly conceivable that Sef, who, as successor to his father at Stanley Falls, was in the closest touch with the Government of the Free State, could have been ignorant of the *rapprochement*

16

between Ngongo Luteta and the Belgians; more especially, the fact that Dhanis had established a station near Ngandu cannot have remained unknown to him, and must have given him matter for reflection. Tippoo Tib's account is obviously the outcome of a desire to relieve his son of the responsibility for events which he himself doubtless deeply regretted.

It has often been contended that Tippoo Tib as Vali of the Congo State always played a double game, but proofs have not yet been adduced of this imputation. When he accepted the appointment offered him by Stanley, he certainly did so with the intention of rescuing whatever was possible in the districts he had once ruled over. That he could not hold these by force of arms against the Belgians as they pressed forward from the West he had long since convinced himself, knowing as he did the superior resources of the Europeans; nor did the temporary successes which during his absence the Arabs achieved in their struggle with the Belgians lead him astray on that head. He knew that after the loss of their station they would come with a fresh military levy, and recover their lost ground with interest. Thus it remained, as matters stood, the most advantageous plan for the Arabs to live at peace with the Europeans as long as they possibly could. There was business enough still to be done in little frequented regions of boundless extent. There was ivory everywhere in rich abundance, and the new masters could not at one blow sweep away the lucrative slave trade.

It was certainly not an easy position which Tippoo Tib occupied as intermediary between the two con-

flicting elements, but the respect he enjoyed among
his countrymen as a member of an old Arab family
and the lord of thousands of slaves, the superior
astuteness with which he always recognised the right
course, and the steadiness of old age, which kept
him from imprudences, enabled him to reconcile
differences that it seemed impossible to bridge over.
Had he not been on the spot for several years as the
vassal of the Congo State, the fire that smouldered
under the ashes would certainly have burst out
sooner.   Let us try to realize the situation : On the
one side the Arabs, the ancient masters of the
country, who for years had carried on a calling which, according to their views, was justifiable ;
on the other, an intruding European Power, which
endeavoured step by step to restrict them in the
exercise of what they conceived to be their fairly
won rights.   The contrasts were too sharp for a
lasting peace to be possible.

As soon as Tippoo Tib left the scene and his
personal influence vanished with him, there was
bound sooner or later to be a catastrophe.   The
Arabs from their standpoint needed no excuse if they
at length took arms ; nor does any reproach attach
to Tippoo Tib's youthful son Sef for allowing himself to be induced by the insistence of the Arabs,
whose most vital interests were affected, to attack
the Belgians.   A day of reckoning between Arabs
and Europeans in those districts was a historical
necessity, which had been postponed through the
influence of a great personality, but could not be
wholly avoided.

Let us, then, leave it an open question whether

16—2

Sef desired war with the Belgians or not; in any case, by his attack on Ngongo Luteta hostilities were commenced, and events took the course which thev were bound to take. ' It was decreed that the matter should end ill,' says the fatalist auto-biographer.

In detail the course of the struggle was as follows : * Sef, for reasons which we will leave undetermined, had attacked Ngongo Luteta. The Belgians, who had received in good time informa-tion of the enemy's intentions, came to the rescue of their new vassal, and Sef and his bands, who had pressed forward to the Lomami, after sharp fighting from November, 1892, to January 11, 1893, were driven back to the Congo. Mwinyi Mohara, who had taken part in the campaign, was killed, and a nephew of Tippoo Tib's, Sef bin Juma, was drowned in the Lomami.

Dhanis, the leader of the Belgian troops, pursued the Arabs, and encamped opposite Nyangwe, on the left bank of the Congo, on January 29, 1893. The river is at that point 120 yards wide, and he could not cross it, for the Arabs had taken all their boats across with them. He therefore contented himself with bombarding the settlements of the Arabs from his side of the stream. The latter, however, rashly assumed the offensive by crossing the river and establishing two camps opposite the position of the Belgians. They were routed by Dhanis after a day's fighting, and had to flee back to the right bank. By this success the Belgians gained the

* *Cf.*, for the sketch that follows, the periodical *Le Mouve-ment Géographique* for February 4, 1884.

sympathies of the natives, who now aided them by bringing to the spot the boats necessary for crossing the stream. On March 4 Nyangwe fell, without further fighting, into Dhanis's hands.

At Kassongo the news of the defeat of the Arabs on the Lomami and the death of Mwinyi Mohara evoked great bitterness. It had been erroneously reported that Tippoo Tib's son had also fallen. Fugitives had, it appears, reported that his *mtoto* (which means son as well as nephew) Sef had lost his life. The Arabs and natives, who at the name Sef thought first of the son of our hero, were convinced that he was a victim of the conflict, and out of revenge murdered the Europeans living in Kassongo.

After giving his troops a short rest at Nyangwe, Dhanis marched against Kassongo on April 17, and captured it, with the help of Ngongo Luteta, on the 22nd of that month, after furious fighting. In wild flight the Arabs abandoned the field, and many of them were drowned in the River Musokoi. A great booty fell into the hands of the victors, amongst other things 3 tons of ivory, 20 hundred-weight of powder, and as many repeating rifles. A lucky find was made here, too, in the discovery of the last leaves of the diary of Emin Pasha, who had been murdered meanwhile.

While the Arabs were thus harried in the southern districts, in the north also Lieutenant Chaltin had conducted an expedition against the insurgents from Basoko, the junction of the Lomami and the Congo. He had steamed up the Congo and the Lomami, had there taken possession, without a

blow, of the settlements of Yangi, Bena, Kamba,
and Lomo, which the Arabs had abandoned, and
finally, on April 22, marched overland to the Arab
station of Riba Riba, on the left bank of the Congo,
which he also found deserted. He rightly reflected
that the fugitive Arabs must have retired to their
headquarters at Stanley Falls, and from Bena
Kamba he proceeded thither on board the steamer
Ville de Bruxelles, which was at his disposal. On the
way, near the mouth of the Lomami, a letter reached
him from Tobbak, the Commandant of Stanley
Falls, which showed that his surmise was quite
correct.

The Arabs there had received intelligence of the
defeats of their compatriots at Nyangwe and Kassongo, and were now gathering all their available
fighting strength to strike a decisive blow at the
Europeans. After various minor skirmishes, the
Dutch factory was attacked during the night of
May 11. Next day the settlement of the Belgian
Upper Congo Company was occupied by the Shensis
in the service of the Arabs, two Government boats
were fired on, and an attack on the station itself
attempted.

Tobbak was holding out with difficulty against
superior numbers, when on the 18th, at the moment
of his greatest extremity, the *Ville de Bruxelles*
drew near with the longed-for relief force under
Chaltin. On its appearance the Arabs took to
flight, and the town remained in the hands of the
Europeans. About the middle of July Commandant
Ponthier, who had returned from leave in Europe,
took the station of Kirundu, above Stanley Falls.

The insurgents suffered a severe defeat: twenty-eight chiefs were taken prisoners and 1,000 rifles fell into the hands of the victors.

Thus the power of the Arabs on the Congo was shattered. Such of them as escaped retreated to Tanganyika, and there joined the forces of Rumalisa, who meanwhile had resumed his baffled plan of attacking the Belgians westward of the lake. As he had some 3,000 rifles at his disposal, he was able for some time to press hard on Captain Jaques, who was in those parts. But the latter summoned reinforcements, and with the help of two officers, Delcommune and Joubert, succeeded, in September, 1892, in driving the Arab partisan back on Albert-ville.

When the fugitives from Kassongo arrived, Rumalisa once more marshalled a strong army, and marched with it to meet the advancing Belgians under Dhanis and Ponthier. On October 20, 1893, a sanguinary engagement took place on the river Luama, ending, after heavy losses on both sides, in a decisive victory for the Europeans. The Belgians lost their commander Ponthier, who a few days later succumbed to wounds received in the action. Tippoo Tib's son Sef also, with numerous other Arabs, paid for the attack with his life.

This blow broke the power of the Arabs westward of Tanganyika as well, and such of the survivors as did not fall into the hands of the victors took their way through German territory back to their homes, and since then have never attempted open resistance to the European power.

In truth in the time that followed this would have been scarcely possible. On July 2, 1890, the Anti-slavery Conference at Brussels had adopted its well-known General Declaration, which, in the endeavour to cope with the ravages of the African slave trade, contained strict regulations as to the trade in fire-arms and ammunition as well. The Belgians, who previously used to sell Tippoo Tib and his people powder in unlimited quantities, now, after the woeful experiences that they had had in the matter, of course stood out for the exact observance of these regulations.

Tippoo Tib was kept *au courant* of all the warlike events in his former province by his adherents, but we may implicitly believe his assurance that he had no share in the hostilities—nay, on the contrary, regretted them. All letters that came in he laid before the German and British Consuls for their information. Through their reports, by the round-about way of Zanzibar, many occurrences were known in Europe before they became officially public via Brussels.

Our hero saw plainly that he could no longer check the course of events, and bore the many losses which befell him personally with the stoical calm of the Muhammedan. The war had cost him 4,500 *frasilas* of ivory, 700 loads of stuff for garments, and 20,000 muskets. He could, however, console himself with the treasures which he had gradually placed in safety. Numerous *shambas* and houses in Zanzibar and on the coast were his property.

But even these were now for the most part to be

subject to dispute. Rumalisa, who escaped with his bare life from the disastrous fights on Tanganyika, had fled by secret ways (for he dreaded the vengeance of the Germans) to the coast, and had been taken across to Zanzibar in a fishing-boat ; he now came forward suddenly with a claim to the effect that Tippoo Tib owed him a quarter of his fortune. He produced a document setting forth that he, Tippoo Tib, and Bwana Nzige had formed a partnership, by which all profits that they might earn were to be divided between them ; Tippoo Tib was to receive a half, the other two a quarter apiece.

Our hero has always disputed the authenticity of this document, as did his cousin Bwana Nzige. They both declared that their signatures appended to it were forgeries. The result was a lengthy lawsuit before the court at Dar-es-Salaam, which Rumalisa won. This decision gave rise to a long contest as to the amount of the quarter to be handed over by Tippoo Tib, ending in a judicial settlement by which Tippoo Tib gave up his whole property on the coast to his opponent, the particular items being specified in an inventory.

It soon proved, however, that various objects of value transferred by him did not exist, amongst others a quantity of ivory supposed to be buried at Itahua, and a claim for a debt of 6,000 dollars. As Tippoo Tib, who is a Zanzibari subject, was no longer liable, after the surrender of his property on the coast, to be sued in the German colony, Rumalisa raised a claim in the Sultan's court for compensation for the valuables not forthcoming. According to the principles obtaining, he was recognised as a German subject, and his plaint was supported by the German Consulate, which took advantage of its treaty rights to have the sittings of the court watched by a representative, and the present writer, to whom this duty was allotted, was thus for the first time enabled to make the acquaintance of the hero of this story, to be sure in somewhat unfriendly wise. After a ' protracted litigation it was at last declared in the court of appeal by the Sultan himself that the defendant, in fulfilment of the settlement, must pay a further sum of 6,000 dollars.

The plaintiff, it must be admitted, was not much the gainer thereby. The sum adjudged him was for the most part swallowed up by the lawyer's fees, and so many creditors were lying in wait for the remainder that soon after his success he announced his bankruptcy, which is still pending before the district court of Dar-es-Salaam. Tippoo Tib consoled himself with the thought that the old proverb, 'Mali ya haramu yanakwenda nyia ya haramu '— Ill-gotten gains never prosper — had once more been verified.

Yet another lawsuit gave the Sheikh a great deal of trouble. The heirs of his business friend Taria Topan, who had died towards the end of the eighties, declared that at the time of his death Tippoo Tib still owed him 15,000 rupees, and brought an action for this sum. The examination of the books ordered by the court showed that, on the contrary, our hero had still 35,000 rupees to receive from his banker. He now 'turned the spear the other way,' and claimed of Taria's grandson, Saleh, who had taken over the business later on, not only the payment of

this amount, but of a further considerable sum which
was due to him from their later business connections.   As a result he not long since obtained a
valid judgment for the not inconsiderable amount
of 300,000 rupees; but he will not set eyes on
much of this money, for Saleh has long since
run through his inheritance from his grandfather.

On the other hand, all this litigation has entailed
heavy sacrifices on our hero.   The English lawyer
who acted for him pocketed the magnificent fee of
20,000 rupees (about £1,350) for his pains.

Tippoo Tib has not again come to the fore
politically since his final return to Zanzibar, but, as
in his earlier years, he has always tried to be on
good terms with the rulers for the time being.
Seyyid Ali, who was ruling on his arrival, had long
been his personal friend, and always treated him
with goodwill, even though, as Tippoo Tib complains, he was avaricious and not over-free with
presents to his favourites.   Hamed bin Thweni,
who succeeded him, was ill-disposed to Tippoo Tib,
because he had once outbid him at the purchase of
a *shamba* on which the Prince had cast his eye.
Not till shortly before Hamed's death were the
relations between them improved.

It is well known that when this Sultan died,
Seyyid Burghash's youthful son Khalid endeavoured
to ascend the throne, contrary to the wish of the
protecting Power.   He garrisoned the palace, and a
whole English squadron was needed to drive him out
of it.   When further resistance proved impossible
the young Prince fled from the building, which was

collapsing over his head, to the German Consulate, and, after finding refuge there for a month, was conveyed across to Dar-es-Salaam in a German man-of-war, where he now lives as the guest of the Empire, and dreams of his past splendour as Sultan.

Tippoo Tib was on terms of most cordial friendship with the energetic and warm-hearted son of his former patron, and honestly strove to restrain him from the folly of bidding defiance with his handful of warriors to a great European Power. In the certainty that such resistance would be unsuccessful, he kept aloof from the struggle, which brought financial ruin on many highly-placed Arabs, whose participation in it was visited by heavy fines.

His cousin Hamud bin Muhammed was appointed Hamed's successor. He formed a close friendship with Tippoo Tib, and always reckoned him one of his confidential advisers. On two journeys which he made to the African mainland the Sheikh was among his few companions.

Since Hamud's death, which took place in 1904, his son Ali, a minor, has been reigning; but he is under the guardianship of the English Premier, and as yet has little say in the affairs of government. As he was brought up in English fashion, he is but little in touch with Arab circles.

Tippoo Tib is, nevertheless, still an important personage in the Council of Zanzibar, and where it is a question of doing something for the country he is one of the first to be asked his views. In his mockingly superior way he is wont on such

occasions to be not at all backward with his opinion.

He knows, however, that the times of Arab glory are past, and possesses no further political ambition. With the youthful activity which he has preserved even into his old age, this man of nearly seventy attends untiringly to his numerous personal affairs. His fortune still amounts to £50,000 in round figures, and is very advantageously invested in stone houses and landed property.

His longing is some day to behold the magic land of Europe, of whose splendour he had a foretaste at Cape Town. A pilgrimage is also still expected of him by Allah, for the Koran lays down that every Moslem whose means admit of it should at least once in his life undertake the journey to the holy city of Mecca.

His idea is to combine the two journeys, and as in his robust old age he still counts on many more years of life, he hopes to be able, sooner or later, to carry out the plan. 'In sha Allah!'

Tippoo Tib died at Zanzibar, of malaria, on June 13, 1905. The death of Wissmann followed on the very next day; that of Stanley had taken place a year earlier. Thus within a brief period of time three of the most striking personalities among those who wrested its secrets from the Dark Continent have passed away.

Dwellers at a distance may find something strange in this juxtaposition of the slave-hunter's name with those of the two world-famed explorers; to one who

has followed the destinies of our hero it will be intelligible enough. Tippoo Tib was no dainty draughtsman, yet the paths traced out by his blood-stained hand have supplied the framework for all the subsequent cartography of German East Africa and the Congo Free State. Thus a life-work of destruction has served to aid the advance of civilization.

THE END